United States-Japanese Relations

United States-Japanese Relations

The 1970's

Edited by Priscilla Clapp

and

Morton H. Halperin

Harvard University Press
Cambridge, Massachusetts, and London, England

327.73052
U5?

Contents

62399

Foreword

In the mid-1960's when Edwin O. Reischauer was the U.S. ambassador to Japan, a group of American scholars under the leadership of John Lindbeck set out for Japan to seek discussions with a similar group of Japanese scholars. Once in Japan, they found that the Japanese style of intellectual exchange was not characterized by group discussion and that Japanese scholars were hesitant to move abruptly in this direction. The Americans had to settle for a series of private meetings with two or three like-minded Japanese scholars at a time.

They returned to Cambridge determined to initiate a series of conferences that would develop a broader intellectual exchange between Japanese and American scholars. The Ford Foundation generously agreed to fund the enterprise and the American Academy of Arts and Sciences undertook its administration. Upon retirement from his post in Tokyo, Edwin O. Reischauer assumed chairmanship of the program and Benjamin H. Brown of the Harvard Center for International Affairs became secretary.

The experiment began in Hawaii in June 1967 and ended in Racine, Wisconsin, in January 1973 some half dozen meetings later. Numerous American and Japanese scholars participated and many aspects of the U.S.–Japanese relationship were explored. By the end of the series, the discussion had become lively and relaxed, and a real dialogue had developed between the Japanese and American participants.

This collection of essays represents the revised papers of the final meeting at Wingspread in January 1973. While each author is clearly expressing his own point of view, the amount of cohesion and balance that exists among these essays is a tribute to the success of the experiment in promoting meaningful dialogue between Japan and the United States. We feel that the book will be a useful contribution to further discussion between Japanese and Americans.

The American participants are grateful to the Japanese scholars who were willing to join in this endeavor. Special thanks go to Shigeharu Matsumoto and Kiichi Saeki for assuming a leadership role and to Fuji Kamiya for arranging and overseeing the production of the Japanese papers.

On behalf of both the American and the Japanese participants, we would like to express our appreciation to those at the Ford Foundation, the American Academy of Arts and Sciences, and the Johnson Foundation who have made these meetings possible.

PAC
MHH

United States-Japanese Relations

1

EDWIN O. REISCHAUER

Introduction:
An Overview

The importance and the vast scale of Japanese-American relations are beyond dispute. The United States and Japan stand first and third in the world in economic production and fourth and sixth in population. Between them has grown up the largest transregional trade the world has ever known. This is paralleled by broader and closer intellectual and cultural contacts than exist between any other major countries with differing cultural backgrounds. The two also have an intimate, even if less happy, strategic relationship. For more than a quarter century, the defense of Japan has depended ultimately on American commitments, while the American strategic position in East Asia and the Western Pacific has centered around American bases in Japan.

Several recent developments, however, have raised doubts about the future of the Japanese-American relationship. The gradual shift from a bipolar to a multipolar world, insofar as this is a reality, suggests the possibility that Japan, one of the five balancing powers heralded in the new situation, will develop an independent if not openly hostile stance toward the United States. The relaxation of tensions and the establishment of closer contacts with China and the Soviet Union on the part of both Japan and the United States has made some people wonder if new alignments might at least in part replace the special Japanese-American relationship. Japan's explosive industrial rise and its inundation of the American market also suggest that growing economic rivalry may sour Japanese-American relations. Long persistent American surpluses in trade with Japan had by 1972 turned into a huge deficit of some four billion dollars, and it proved necessary to carry out two major devaluations of the American dollar against the Japanese yen in quick succession between late 1971 and early 1973. Growing competition between the United States and Japan over markets and resources in other parts of the world also is putting new strains on their relationship. The oil crisis that struck in the autumn of 1973 produced sharply conflicting initial responses in the two countries—the United States emphasizing its determination to be self-sufficient and the Japanese, in their desperate need for oil, bowing to Arab political pressures despite American disapproval. An economic recession in either country resulting from the energy crisis or even increased economic fears could prove seriously disruptive to their relationship.

This is clearly a time of significant transition in Japanese-American relations, but the question is how great the changes will be and in what direction they will lead. Are the prospects as alarming as some would argue, or is there more reason for hope? My own overall judgment would be on the side of cautious optimism. Of course, a drastic shift in Japanese-American relations, leading to very unpleasant and even dangerous conditions for both countries, can by no means be ruled out, but it seems far from inevitable. In fact, the overall forecast might be for some stormy weather but no great change in course.

Despite serious economic frictions, Japanese-American economic relations are likely to remain massive, mutually beneficial, and steadily expanding. It cannot be denied that anxieties over the Japanese invasion of certain American markets could set off a political reaction that produced broadly restrictionist policies. This, in turn, could lead to a trade war between the two countries and thus start a turning of the tide from the free-trade policies of recent decades to worldwide protectionism. But that would be a catastrophe for both countries and the whole world. Such developments are certainly avoidable. The interests of both the United States and Japan lie clearly in the continuation and expansion of the present system of relatively free trade throughout the world. This being the case, the two could easily devise temporary measures to smooth over specific frictions as these arise between them. In the long run, moreover, the inevitable rise of Japanese prices and the predictable slowing down of the Japanese economy will ease the pressures caused by the great discrepancy in economic growth rates between the two countries that has characterized the past two decades.

No one can deny that a sharpening of competition over worldwide natural resources could all too easily produce great new tensions throughout the world. These might be not only between the industrialized consuming countries and the less developed nations but also between industrialized countries like Japan that are extremely poor in resources and those like the United States that are closer to self-sufficiency and are themselves major exporters of natural resources. At the same time, the United States and Japan do share fundamentally similar interests in their need for energy and other resources, in their dependence on a worldwide economic system of relatively free trade, and in their relationship with the developing nations. Cooperation between them and with the other industrialized nations is a much more sensible policy than unbridled competition and rivalry.

Despite increased trade and fuller contacts with China and

the Soviet Union, a major realignment of economic, political, or strategic relationships between these countries and Japan and the United States seems improbable. The autarkic economic policies and self-isolating social and political systems of China and the Soviet Union are likely to limit their economic, cultural, and political relations with both Japan and the United States to levels far below those that exist between the latter two. For example, trade is likely to remain at least five to ten times higher between Japan and the United States than it is between either of them and China or the Soviet Union.

An even more important point is that American and Japanese concepts of world order, international economic relations, and a desirable domestic social and political system are almost certain to remain much more compatible with each other than with the comparable ideologies of either China or the Soviet Union. While the closeness of the relations of Japan or the United States with either China or the Soviet Union could strain their respective relations with the other of the latter pair, it seems highly unlikely that such closeness could damage relations between Japan and the United States. On the contrary, the better their relations are with China and the Soviet Union, the fewer might be the causes for strain in their relations with each other. And even if Japan and the United States should drift apart for other reasons, neither is likely to develop a relationship with China or the Soviet Union that could be a substitute for their present relationship with each other.

Strategic matters have always been the area of greatest tension in Japanese-American relations. Although the Mutual Security Treaty has been accepted almost without question in the United States, the Japanese have had a more ambivalent attitude toward it, viewing it for the most part as no better than a necessary evil. There have been several reasons for this negative estimate. The Security Treaty has meant the existence in Japan of American military bases, which to the Japanese were irritating enclaves of people of sharply different language, culture, and race. It has seemed to involve Japan in an American foreign policy that appeared to most Japanese to be too aggressive and adventuristic, if not entirely nefarious. Worst of all, it has seemed to many Japanese to place their country in a role of subserviency to the United States in foreign policy. Most Japanese all along have wished to see the strategic relationship with the United States lessened, if not entirely eliminated. Differences of opinion have largely been over the speed with which this should be achieved and whether the defense bond should be entirely severed or simply attenuated. The surge of national self-confidence resulting from Japan's spectacular economic success in recent years has made the need for change seem all the more pressing.

These tides of opinion in Japan are paralleled by American desires since the Vietnam disaster to reduce American military involvement in Asia. Some shift in the defense relationship therefore does seem probable, but much less change than some people expect. For one thing, American and Japanese views on security matters have become much closer in recent years than they were before. The American rapprochement with China, the abandonment of a tight containment policy, and the at least partial military withdrawal from Southeast Asia have brought American strategic policies much more in line with Japanese estimates of defense needs.

An even more important point is that for Japan the alternatives to a defense relationship with the United States are not at all attractive. Once opponents of the Security Treaty could assume that the alternative to it would be a Japanese policy of "unarmed neutrality," but this concept has gradually

faded. It was based on two assumptions that are now seen to
be invalid. One was that, even without the treaty, the United
States would remain as the major military power in the
Western Pacific, giving Japan adequate protection regardless
of Japan's own posture. The other was that a relatively
insignificant Japan could choose to remain aloof from serious
world tensions. Japan's economic success instead has made
Japan a major shaper of the world's future and thus the
object not of benign neglect by other countries but of international pressures. At the same time, the United States,
feeling itself overextended in its world role and perceiving
Japan's friendship and security to be the chief American
interest in East Asia, is not likely to maintain a major
strategic position in the area without Japanese cooperation.

This leaves as the alternatives to a Japanese-American defense relationship either a substitute alliance with China or
the Soviet Union or a considerable increase in Japan's own
defense efforts. The first seems highly unrealistic, and in any
case the last thing the Japanese wish to do is to become
embroiled in the Sino-Soviet confrontation. Large-scale rearmament would also pose serious problems. Domestic opposition to it could tear Japan apart politically. It also would
terrify all Japan's neighbors, who already show great anxiety
over her overwhelming economic power. The result thus
would be a great heightening of tensions in East Asia.

It is conceivable that a drift toward rearmament in Japan
could gain enough momentum over time to carry it all the
way to a nuclear position. In physical terms, Japan is capable
of achieving a nuclear potential rather rapidly, and it has
always kept this option open by developing the basic nuclear
know-how and rocketry. Some Japanese even seem to believe
that the possession of a nuclear potential is the only way
Japan can win international recognition as the great nation it
actually is. But there are strong forces militating against

Japan taking this road. Popular sentiments against nuclear weapons continue to run extremely high in Japan. A Japanese bid for nuclear status would probably create dangerous counter pressures and might set off a hazardous wave of nuclear proliferation in the world. In any case, the narrow geographic extent of the Japanese islands and their tremendous concentrations of population suggest that an independent Japanese nuclear force would in fact give far less security to Japan than the more broadly based American nuclear umbrella.

One must conclude that Japan, after all, has no satisfactory substitute for some form of shared defense with the United States. Still, changing attitudes and conditions do call for substantial modifications in this relationship. Clearly the Japanese sense of subordination to the United States must somehow be eliminated. Perhaps this can best be done by having Japan rather than the United States take the lead in defining the nature and needs of the alliance. Since the Japanese have little sense of an immediate threat and Americans of late have become less worried about strategic concerns in Asia, American bases in Japan could probably be reduced to a considerable extent. In point of fact, such a reduction would be merely a continuation or acceleration of a process that has been going on for two decades. The remaining bases might even be returned to Japan and used by American forces only under agreement for specific purposes. Thus even in the strategic field the problems are by no means insoluble, if there is a desire on both sides to overcome them. A drastic shift even in this most troubled aspect of the Japanese-American relationship seems on the whole unlikely.

The preceding analysis would suggest that no great changes should be expected in the Japanese-American relationship and that there is no reason for alarm. But is this actually the case? In both countries there is great uneasiness about the other, highlighted in the United States by irritation and anxiety over economic matters and in Japan by deep resentments as well as doubts over the defense relationship. This uneasiness is not just limited to the general uninformed public. It appears to be felt most strongly by those who know most about Japanese-American relations.

There may be no reason for any great change in the relationship so long as both sides have the will to solve the many specific problems that constantly come up, but the real question is whether such a will exists—or rather, whether there is enough understanding on both sides of attitudes in the other country to make clear the need for determined efforts to alleviate the frictions between them and whether there are enough skills in communication on both sides to work out solutions. In other words, difficulties in understanding and communication lie at the core of the problem.

In both countries there is a tendency to see the mutual relationship as being unequal, but in opposite ways. Each side sees itself as somehow victimized by the other. Americans feel that, in contrast to the economic generosity they showed a defeated and pauperized Japan after the war, the Japanese in recent years have been insensitive to American economic problems, being much too slow in opening their country in reciprocal fashion to American goods and investments and disrupting sections of the American market by unfair if not clearly illegal trade practices. They feel that Japan has taken a "free ride" on American defense policies, profiting from the costly American nuclear umbrella, the American military presence in the Western Pacific, its commitment to the security of South Korea next door to Japan, its well-meaning even if sometimes misguided efforts to maintain stability in East Asia, and its leadership role in aid to the developing countries. Japan, in return, they feel, has minimized its own role in both defense and aid, while giving at best only grudging support to American policies and indulging in loud public criticism of almost every American move.

Both in Washington and in the country as a whole there is considerable sentiment that the time has come to stop pampering Japan, to be tough with it in economic dealings, and to demand of it a role in the world commensurate with its wealth. This was certainly the message that came through to the Japanese from President Nixon's foreign policy message of May 3, 1973. Some Americans even lean to the view, prevalent in Western Europe, that the Japanese are so alien— that is, so different in their economic ways and basic attitudes—that they must be treated in a separate and discriminatory manner from other industrialized nations.

In Japan all these matters appear in a very different light. The Japanese, living under very crowded conditions in a narrow land with few natural resources, see themselves as still poor and their economy as precariously dependent on foreign resources and markets. In short, Japan, they believe, still merits special economic consideration. For them, the Security Treaty carries heavy psychological and political costs, because of the presence of foreign bases and the resultant sense of subserviency to the United States in foreign policy. They also feel that the treaty has been mostly in the interests of the United States in furthering its somewhat suspect objectives in East Asia. Some even believe that Japan has been as much endangered as protected by the treaty, because it has involved Japan in America's bellicose and adventuristic Far Eastern policies. Even some of those who supported the treaty in the past are beginning to have doubts about its value in the future. They wonder if the ambiguities of the Nixon Doctrine do not reveal that Japan, as an Asian country, cannot depend on an American defense commitment with the same assurance as would a Western country. Still worse,

they fear that history and ingrained Western arrogance may
make Americans incapable of treating Japanese as real equals
in defense relations. Similarly, they wonder if American and
European reactions to Japan's economic success do not show
that Westerners are unwilling to grant Japanese equal treatment even in the field of economics.

If there were full and easy communication between Japan
and the United States, such misunderstandings and differences of viewpoint might be ironed out or at least minimized.
But this unfortunately is not the case. Communication between the two countries is far from adequate. This is an
aspect of the problem that perhaps should have received
more emphasis than it does in this volume, especially since
the series of meetings that led up to its publication was itself
a very successful effort to bridge the communication gap.

There are a number of reasons for the inadequacy of
communication between the two countries. The simple language barrier itself cannot be overemphasized. Relatively few
Japanese, especially as compared with the citizens of other
industrialized nations with comparably close relations with
the United States, handle the English language with ease and
accuracy, and Americans who speak and read Japanese are a
rarity. Translations between the two languages are often
grossly inaccurate in connotation, if not in specific statement. Oral interpretation is likely to be even more mislead-
ing. The translators and interpreters themselves should not be
blamed for this sorry situation so much as the great differences between the two languages. Anyone who knows both is
continually dismayed by the way the gold of the one seems
to be transformed into the dross of the other.

Another problem is the difference in the styles of communication. Accustomed for centuries to life in a crowded but
culturally homogeneous land, the Japanese have developed
habits of communication by indirection and understatement.

It has seemed important to them to avoid open confrontation, and thus they tend to negotiate through intermediaries or to approach their bargaining goal by slow and tentative steps. Americans by contrast like to stake out from the start their maximum bargaining position. Their assertiveness seems unreasonable to Japanese; Japanese caution seems devious to Americans. Even with full linguistic comprehension, real communication may not take place because of the great difference in wave lengths of the two communicators. It is perhaps because of factors of this sort that we witness the strange phenomenon of President Nixon and Henry Kissinger communicating with apparent ease and pleasure with the Chinese leaders but finding communication with their close allies, the Japanese leaders, both difficult and distasteful.

Contrasts in cultural background, historical experience, and basic assumptions can constitute even more serious bars to comprehension, and to these should be added the great disparity in attention Japanese and Americans pay to each other. For the past two decades, Americans have been relatively oblivious of Japan, in part because the Japanese have preferred to maintain a "low posture" in international affairs in order to concentrate on their own economic recovery. Even today, when Japan's spectacular success has shoved her into the limelight, Americans remain surprisingly unaware of Japanese attitudes and sensitivities. On the other hand, the large role the United States has played in Japan's fate ever since World War II has made Japanese overly conscious of every American word or act. Incidents in Japanese-American relations that the American mass media overlook completely can lead to screaming headlines in Japan. An offhand comment on the American side can produce a violent and bitter reaction in Japan, which in turn is scarcely noticed in the United States. Here again communication is not on the same wave length.

The causes for discord in Japanese-American relations are much less basic than the reasons for harmony and cooperation. The problem seems more a matter of understanding than of fundamental conflicts of interest. But this does not make it any the less real. A growing estrangement between the two countries is by no means inconceivable and, if it were to materialize, great harm could be done to both and to the whole world.

A deterioration in economic relations would be economically injurious to both sides and would run the risk of setting off a broader trade war and a retreat from global trade patterns to less advantageous regional ones. This in turn might entail the breakup or at least the weakening of the emerging community of the major industrialized nations of Western Europe, North America, and Japan, which at present gives promise of becoming the nucleus of an eventual world community. Divided into regional blocs, these countries would become less able to cope with rising global problems, such as world-wide pollution, the growing imbalance between limited natural resources and mounting populations, a need for more rational and dependable allocation of the resources of the world, and the widening gap in per capita income between the affluent minority in the already industrialized nations and the poor, dissatisfied majority in most of the developing countries. If this gap continues to grow as the globe goes on shrinking in size and international relations become ever more complex, the result could be such political instability in the world as to threaten all civilization. There is a desperate need to develop much greater skills in handling such global problems, but a drifting apart of the major actors, such as the United States and Japan, would mean a decline in the capacity for effective cooperation.

Even in the narrower framework of East Asia, an estrangement between Japan and the United States would be frightening. The Japanese, feeling economically rejected by the countries of the West and losing confidence in the defense relationship with the United States, would probably feel that they must concentrate their economic efforts all the more on their neighboring countries and also put somewhat more emphasis on developing their own military power. Both steps would greatly alarm their neighbors, who already are disturbed over Japan's preponderant economic might in the region and remember her as the great military conqueror of a generation ago. Tensions would probably mount throughout East Asia, a dangerous hostility between China and Japan might be set in motion, and in time serious rivalry with the Soviet Union and even with the United States might ensue.

These are all distressing prospects, but are they not largely chimerical, since they are based more on psychological tensions than on basic clashes of interest? Perhaps so. All the forces of economics and all the persuasiveness of rational thought push in the opposite direction. But the human record for flouting reason and real interests is by no means comforting. And there are at present specific conditions within both the United States and Japan that make the overcoming of these psychological hazards all the more difficult.

On the American side, there is need for much greater awareness of Japan, more sensitivity to Japanese attitudes and fears, and far more determined efforts to overcome the barriers to communication and understanding. Instead we find a country in a mood of frustration over a disaster abroad and a multiplicity of problems at home. Swinging from hubris, it has plunged into self-doubt. After a generation of arrogant self-confidence as the self-appointed savior of a war-torn world and arbiter of global destinies, it has turned inward. It feels economically disadvantaged by others, particularly the Japanese. It is insistent that others share more fully in the international load it has been carrying. It dwells on the need for Japan to show itself more responsive to American problems and demands, without realizing that reciprocal efforts by the United States are also required.

Much of this shift in American attitude is justified. The United States clearly has been too self-confident; it does need to devote more attention to domestic problems; and other countries, notably those of Western Europe and Japan, should be more sensitive to American difficulties and should perhaps assume more of the international responsibilities that the United States has attempted to carry too long by itself. But the change in mood could easily carry the United States to excesses on the other side. The situation with regard to Japan is especially dangerous. However justified some American demands may be, there is still a great need for Americans to try to understand Japan better and to devote much greater efforts to overcoming the barriers to communication.

Unfortunately there is little sign of this happening. Instead, popular prejudices against Japan flare up easily over specific and often relatively minor economic issues, while the administration in Washington is almost blatantly oblivious to Japanese feelings. This was illustrated most clearly in 1971 at the time of the spectacular step toward rapprochement with China, when Japanese sentiments were entirely disregarded and all past promises of full consultation and close cooperation with Japan over China policy were simply ignored. It is no wonder that the Japanese have called this incident the "Nixon shock." Even after this blunder, the White House continued to see no need to have expert knowledge on Japan, even though it had taken care to build up competent staffs of Soviet and Chinese experts. While working assiduously for better communication with the Chinese and Russians, it continued to give only pro forma attention to communication with the Japanese, accepting the difficulty of dealing with the Japanese leaders and the lack of empathy with them as sufficient reason for not trying harder.

The situation in Japan is perhaps even more distressing. If there is to be a healthy Japanese-American relationship, the time has certainly come for Japan both to be more sensitive to American attitudes and to speak forth more clearly and assertively about its own desires with regard to the American relationship and the role it intends to play in the world. In fact, Japan should have started to act in this way some years ago. Instead it has permitted irritations to grow in the United States and in the world over Japan's apparent willingness to take advantage of the policies of other countries without taking any clear stands itself. At the same time, its timid and purely reactive foreign policies have allowed frustrations to grow among the Japanese public over Japan's apparent continuing subservience to the United States. Japan can no longer play the role simply of reluctant reactor to the initiatives of others. Such a stance for the third largest economic power in the world has become psychologically unsound for the Japanese themselves and unacceptable to Americans and other peoples, who expect more than this from a vigorous and spectacularly successful Japan.

To put the problem in more specific terms, a healthy Japanese-American relationship can only be one that is felt on both sides to be equal, and for this there must be real mutuality and full and open communication. For example, if the ticklish defense relationship is to be put on a sound basis, the Japanese government should make clear to its own people as well as to the United States what it seeks from the alliance. In its economic relation with the United States and the other industrialized nations, Japan needs to move more rapidly and forcefully to head off economic frictions before they get out of hand politically. In its relations with its neighbors and with other developing nations, it needs to make clear and concrete its willingness to play a larger part in economic aid and a more positive role in international cooperation in general. Such actions would force Americans and others to pay greater attention to Japan, would help dispel their present irritation with Japan, and would free the Japanese public from their nagging sense of being disdained by the world as self-seeking "economic animals" and a mere satellite of the United States.

This may be what Japan should do, but there is little sign that she will. The nation has become set in its habits of avoiding international initiatives and merely reacting to what develops elsewhere. The policy of maintaining a "low posture" and concentrating on its own economic growth did fit Japan's situation as a relatively poor and weak country during the first two decades after the war, and it proved spectacularly successful then. It is hard for the Japanese to see that, now that their country is an economic giant, this posture will work no longer and is in fact leading Japan into serious dangers. But even if there were more widespread understanding in Japan of the need for a change in approach, the prognosis would still not be very hopeful.

As Masataka Kosaka persuasively argues in the following chapter, there is little chance that the Japanese government will be able to make rapid and bold decisions on such matters. The Japanese dislike positive, charismatic leadership in politics, preferring instead a more diffuse system of decision making, in which a powerful bureaucracy plays a dominant role. Bureaucratic leadership, however, tends inevitably toward policy inertia, because policies once adopted produce strong bureaucratic momentum and thus tend to continue unaltered. The Japanese also have a strong yearning for consensus, which requires slow and protracted consultations, rather than sharp and quick majority decisions, which they call the "tyranny of the majority." This attitude, when combined with the deep cleavage between left and right, particularly over foreign policy issues, means that the opposition left has a virtual veto power over the conservative government on such matters. All this may give Japanese politics an admirable degree of stability, but it makes Japanese foreign policy distressingly immobile.

At a time that demands positive action and a decided change in stance on the part of Japan, this immobility could be tragic. Japan's economic success has given rise to a long delayed but now very strong sense of national self-confidence and pride. The bitter experiences of World War II and its aftermath still make most Japanese hesitant to express these feelings in blatantly nationalistic terms, but they are nonetheless strong. The combination of disregard and irritation that characterizes the attitudes of Americans, Europeans, and even some Asians toward Japan is becoming increasingly galling to Japanese. But the Japanese government may prove unable to take the sort of action that could both diminish foreign irritation and increase national respect. If that is true, Japanese nationalism, lacking positive means of expression, may turn increasingly to negative manifestations. In Japan the most obvious and simplest way to express frustrations over international affairs is through anti-American agitation. All along this has constituted the largest single expression of popular attitudes on foreign policy matters. If this situation continues and grows worse, Japanese-American relations could be seriously damaged, to the great disadvantage of Japan almost at once, but with serious effects over the long run for the United States and the whole world.

This chapter, in delineating in broad outline what is involved in Japanese-American relations, has put considerable emphasis on the disastrous consequences that might follow from a serious breakdown in these relations. It is not meant to be interpreted, however, as a prediction that any of this will necessarily happen. At present the reasons to expect continuing friendship and cooperation seem clearly to outweigh the reasons to expect disaster. But it is well to realize what all the possibilities are. If we are aware of the surrounding precipices, we can better appreciate the character of the political and economic terrain in which we now find ourselves and the significance of the paths that lie ahead. The chapters that follow show in more detail some of the salient features of this surrounding terrain and the paths that lead through it.

2

MASATAKA KOSAKA

Political Immobility and the Uncertain Future

The author of the best-selling novel *The Japanese and the Jews* under the pen name Isaiah Ben-Dasan has provided an ironical description of the character of Japanese politics.[1] He writes that "everything is very irrational and unfair but everything is amicably settled." He also suggests that there is "political genius" in Japan's ability to maintain political stability in the face of surprising change. But his ironic style gives the impression that he may really be warning of the danger in Japanese politics, despite the apparent successes of the past two decades.

It is true that Japanese politics have shown remarkable stability since the beginning of the 1950's. With the single exception of Prime Minister Tanzan Ishibashi (who resigned because of illness), postwar prime ministers in Japan have enjoyed relatively long tenures in office, in sharp contrast to the prewar days when most tenures were short-lived. This has produced fairly consistent policies in both foreign and domestic affairs. Outwardly, the stability of politics and consistency of policies have had beneficial effects on Japan. But is the stability real? Is the consistency not due to the fact that Japan is prevented both internally and externally from

taking any initiatives? In a word, this consistency may really
be immobility. If so, there is a latent possibility of some
radical change in the future, as is often the case with an
immobile political system.

THE ORIGINS OF JAPANESE POLITICAL IMMOBILITY

There are three major reasons for describing the Japanese
political system as immobile, or at least inactive:

1. The decline of the LDP. The position of the Liberal
Democratic party (LDP) is not so strong as its majority of
300 out of 486 seats in the House of Representatives might
suggest. It is true that voters have given the LDP nearly 300
seats in every election since its creation in 1955, but they
have done so somewhat unwillingly because there is no viable
alternative to the LDP. During the 1960's for example, the
position of the LDP slowly but steadily declined: while it
gained 57.5 percent of the total vote in the 1960 election, it
won only 46.8 percent in the 1972 election.[2] This decline is
attributed mainly to the flow of population from rural areas,
which form the center of LDP power, to urban areas, where
the LDP is not so popular.

At the beginning of the 1960's, an important member of
the LDP forecast that the party would lose its majority in
the course of the 1960's and be overtaken by the Socialist
party.[3] The forecast proved to be true as far as the votes for
the LDP were concerned, but its predictions for the ascen-
dency of the JSP were not fulfilled. Toward the end of the
1960's the JSP's electoral support began to decline and
eventually leveled off at a rather low ceiling.

Poor human resources and a lack of pragmatic policies,
symbolized by advocacy of unarmed neutrality, probably
account in large part for the JSP's failure to gain the nation's
confidence. Because the JSP has no hope of gaining power in

the foreseeable future, it cannot recruit able people. Without this broader capability the party is forced to assert its existence by proclaiming the most radical platform. This ensures some support, but the very radicalness of the platform keeps the support from expanding. And if the radical platform were modified, the support would disappear. In other words, the JSP must exist as a veto group and nothing more.

Thus, the Japanese electorate must cast its vote for the LDP, because it is the only party that appears able to govern the country. The electorate's support for the LDP at the polls does not necessarily indicate support for the policies of the LDP. Basically, the LDP wins votes because its members attend closely to the specific interests of their constituents. The most common practice is for Diet members to pass the specific demands of their electors on to those who decide policy—the government and the bureaucrats.[4] This pattern of action may not appear unique, but the fact that Diet members are elected almost exclusively by virtue of this activity is certainly unique. Thus, voters cast their ballots on the basis of more immediate self-interest and are relatively indifferent to national policies.

2. Lack of consensus. Given the relative lack of interest in national policy, it is no wonder that there has been no consensus on the most fundamental policy issues. The LDP has failed to create a consensus, a situation that is especially apparent in foreign policy. Public opinion has been split since the U.S.–Japanese Peace Treaty of 1951, the focus of the disagreement being Japan's security relationship with the United States. The LDP has asserted that cooperation with the United States and the "free world" should be the guiding principle of Japan's foreign policy, while the opposition has continued to demand the abrogation of the U.S.–Japanese Mutual Security Treaty and the adoption of neutrality.[5] The opposition parties are against strengthening military coopera-

tion with the United States or even economic assistance to
Southeast Asia within the American framework.

Japan's foreign policy can be considered a product of the
uneasy balance between government policy and opposition
views. The conservative party continues to hold a majority
mainly because it promotes the tangible interests of the
inhabitants, but the foreign policy of that party's government
does not have the general support of the people. Although
the opposition parties' arguments are too impractical to form
a majority opinion, they can serve as a very effective veto
group.

This basic pattern leaves Japan with a foreign policy that is
either inactive or negative. For example, the existence of this
strong opposition has led the government to take a very
passive stand on security problems and to pursue a vague
defense policy, to the consternation of the United States.
Only recently have the leaders of the governing party begun
to argue with conviction for Japanese-American security ties
and other measures necessary for Japan's safety. The persis-
tence of the opposition's influence on basic policy is indeed
remarkable and is not something that would be manifest in a
stable political system.

The split over domestic policy seems now to hinge on the
strength and nature of the state's power, with the conservatives proclaiming an "etatist" philosophy[6] and the opposition parties arguing against any expansion of state power. In
a sense, the conservatives represent a traditional Japanese
tendency to equate modernization with a strong central government that dates back to the Meiji Restoration. The Japanese people in general entertain an ambivalent attitude
toward "etatism." On the one hand, they regard a strong
central government as necessary and they depend on its
services. On the other hand, they are uneasy about the
government's centralized power.

At election time this ambivalence manifests itself in a permanent victory for the government party and vocal support for the opposition. This pattern persists in Japanese political life. During the twentieth century, the opposition parties in Japan have never won an election, with two doubtful exceptions.[7] Nevertheless, the opposition has enjoyed general popularity. It is not difficult to see that the balance between the need for strong central government and feelings against it can push political action toward a position of immobility. Both the LDP and the opposition parties are not satisfied with the present state of affairs, but they can do little to change it.

3. The defects of consensus decision making. Japanese society relies more than any other on consensus in order to act. Consensus decision making consists roughly of a series of lengthy meetings in which issues are discussed in a very vague and noncommittal way until gradually an opinion begins to form around what seems to be the group's common denominator. Usually the process is presided over by a father figure, who serves as a middleman and lends his authority in announcing the decision.

Some people find assets in this system, others find liabilities. Clearly, it has several advantages. As Herman Kahn argues, it enables the mobilization of the energies of the society; it promotes a sense of participation as it enlists the opinions of the constituent members; it precludes the appearance of a "maverick" once the decision has been reached; and execution is expedited because most understand the decision thoroughly and feel committed to it through their participation.[8]

However, it also has several disadvantages. It is time consuming, not only because it requires so many meetings, but also because it is difficult to overrule opposing views. The

Japanese are not happy with simple majority decisions.[9] A consensus decision must to some extent satisfy the desires of nearly everyone and at least, not ignore anyone completely. Therefore, a convinced or stubborn minority can block a decision or delay it for a long time. Consensus decision making tends to encourage a system of mutual irresponsibility that results in confusion. Because the system is based on consensus, the responsibility and competence of the leaders and those being led is not clearly defined. Everyone tends to be evasive when faced with responsibility for an unpleasant decision. As Zbigniew Brzezinski points out in *Fragile Blossom,* such defects were apparent in Japanese government decision making during World War II.[10] Furthermore, it is difficult to get a clear-cut decision in complex cases, because the facade of consensus must be maintained. The solution is usually found in a vague formula that does not prescribe definite action and tends to compound confusion in the long run.[11]

Obviously, a full understanding of the problems inherent in a consensus system would require more extensive examination, but it is clear that Japan's unique decision-making process has been an important factor contributing to political inaction and immobilism. To state the problem more concretely, it places major obstacles in the way of rational policy making. Even with its clear majority, the LDP can seldom force policy. If the minority were overridden by majority rule, the majority would be severely criticized for disregarding the views of the minority. Naturally, it becomes necessary on occasion for the majority to act against the minority's wishes in order to avoid complete paralysis, but if this happens too often or too blatantly a very strong public reaction sets in. The most outstanding example of this process occurred in 1960 when Prime Minister Kishi forced the ratification of the renegotiated Security Treaty by introducing the police to break the Socialists' blockade of the Diet chamber.

However, the immobility of the Japanese decision-making process has been felt more consistently in the less formal, but more important, decision interaction among the LDP, government bureaucracy, and business. Besides the time required to coordinate the three, there is considerable factionalism within the groups. Tendencies toward factionalism are particularly strong in the LDP and the bureaucracy, who must first develop an internal consensus before dealing with outside groups. It is no wonder that the LDP and the bureaucracy have rarely produced imaginative policies in spite of the high quality of their membership.

JAPAN'S POLITICAL FUTURE

What effects can the immobilist structure be expected to have on Japanese politics in the coming years? This question acquires even more significance when viewed in light of the changes in the world political situation that occurred around 1971. Outwardly, Japan has been cast into a new world role with political and economic responsibilities that were not previously apparent. Inwardly, the Japanese electorate has begun to shift its political allegiances, and in the shuffle, the parties are beginning to play on the nationalist themes that are emerging from the Japanese public attitude toward foreign policy.

Diplomatic initiative. The major characteristics of Japan's postwar foreign policy have been low posture, emphasis on economic development and trade, security dependence on the United States, and the utmost caution in the conduct of foreign affairs to avoid giving offense. This type of policy suited Japan magnificently in the days of the cold war and

American hegemony. The United States was generally dependable, bold diplomatic initiatives were ruled out by the East-West confrontation, and concentration on economic development was safe and profitable. In this world, political immobilism in Japan was no disadvantage. On the contrary, it kept Japan from making any binding commitments.

In the "multipolar" world, however, Japan is now required to take certain diplomatic initiatives. Japan is also expected to share responsibility for management of the world economic system, by virtue of its large GNP and vast international economic activities. In short, Japan cannot now remain inactive and immobilism is beginning to pose serious problems.

To a large extent, these problems are manifest in the weakness of the Japanese political system under conditions of stress and crisis, where quick and bold action is usually required. Although real crisis conditions are unlikely to materialize for Japan as long as the world situation remains basically stable, Japan nonetheless remains in a disadvantageous position should any destabilization demand a rapid decision.

Perhaps the most unfortunate aspects of the Japanese system are its inability to act with foresight and its closed nature.[12] When the task to be done is clear, consensus evolves quite easily. Thus the Japanese are best at adapting or reacting to pressure from outside. But when the situation is not clear-cut, consensus is difficult to achieve. While long-range decisions pose problems for any country, they are even more difficult in Japan.

The current world economic situation, in particular, demands Japanese initiatives. But economic measures must be planned with foresight and usually take effect slowly. A case in point is the liberalization of Japan's import restrictions.

Many in Japan were cognizant of the need for liberalization long before the balance of payments became so preponderantly favorable to Japan. They also recognized that liberalization would be in the best interest of Japan in the long run. However, because liberalization was an immediate threat to some, the decision to liberalize became complex and time-consuming. The farmers and small entrepreneurs who opposed liberalization were a clear minority, but together with the Ministry of Agriculture and the Ministry of International Trade and Industry they were a convinced minority that could not easily be overruled. The result was that action on liberalization came late and the delay probably destroyed chances of reorganizing the structure of the Japanese economy to best adapt it to liberalized import policies.

Another unfortunate aspect of the Japanese political system is its insensitivity to demands from without and its oversensitivity to demands from within. It becomes almost impossible to compromise or sacrifice a minor domestic interest to accommodate the outside world, because the first priority is to obtain consensus within the country. In some cases, if a large majority felt that accommodation were clearly necessary, a sacrifice might be demanded, but this is not the nature of economic matters. In economic relations many different interests are so intricately balanced among the nations and among the several groups within one country that accommodation can only be a very complex process of give-and-take. While the above difficulties may not be peculiar to Japan,[13] one must admit that the Japanese system is less open to outside influence than most other systems. Her geographical position, the homogeneity of her society and her long history of isolation in the Tokugawa era may be principal reasons for Japan's insularity. But the absence of a national sense of Japan's role in the world, the fact that the

old nationalist myth was destroyed by World War II to be
replaced by none, has made the Japanese more domestic-
oriented than ever.

Party politics and nationalism. Thus we come to the problem of nationalism in Japan. The passive foreign policy of
Japan since the war has been a sharp and somewhat puzzling
contrast to the earlier image of the Japanese as a basically
nationalistic people. Actually, the Japanese themselves have
not been satisfied with Japan's passive foreign policy and the
plea for "positive" or "independent" policy has been repeated so often that it has become a cliche. But the plea has
produced little result.

The reasons why Japanese nationalism has failed to produce a more self-assertive foreign policy are twofold. On the
one hand, the Japanese people took a lesson from the failures
of prewar nationalistic policy and feel that Japan must assert
itself in other ways. On the other hand, opinion in Japan
remains divided on exactly how to express this self-assertion.
The government and the LDP, both of which are pragmatic
and conscious of Japan's vulnerability in many senses, think
that Japan can best assert its influence through cooperation
with the United States. It is no wonder that their inclination
to follow the lead has not resulted in Japanese initiatives.
Those in opposition to government policy feel that the true
way lies elsewhere, but they have not been able to reach
agreement on a positive plan of their own. The opposition's
argument is negative in a double sense: both against military
forces and against the United States (or military cooperation
with the United States). One argument appeals to pacifism
and the other to nationalism, wherein the opposition's case
rests.

Thus the lack of consensus over foreign policy can be
described as a difference of opinion over how Japan should
assert itself. When those who advocate following the U.S.

lead are in opposition to the nationalistic negativists, little room is left for constructive initiatives, and the resulting stalemate tends to frustrate the nationalistic desire for positive foreign policy. The danger of such a situation increases as Japan's economic power stimulates a more assertive mood in Japan. However, the memory of the dangers inherent in an assertive foreign policy is still an important safeguard.

The future of Japanese nationalism and foreign policy hinges on the answers to two questions. Will the domestic situation become so chaotic and frustrating that the appeal to nationalism can carry the day? Will the international situation allow Japan to assert itself constructively? Future prospects do not necessarily seem bright.

In the first place, the political situation in Japan will enter an unstable period during the 1970's. Theoretically, the LDP could reverse the decline of its power base during the 1970's by adapting its policies to appeal to the urban population, but this is unlikely to occur successfully in the near future. The LDP represents rural society not only by looking after its interests but also by reflecting its behavioral characteristics. The LDP style that appeals to the rural population often repels urban society. Rather than adapting its appeal to urban voters, the LDP's reaction has been to rely even more on the farmers' support.[14] This has resulted in conservative economic policies and a continuing decline in the LDP's strength.

At the same time, the JSP has also been declining in strength because of its inability to overcome the problems mentioned earlier. Adherence to a doctrinaire theory of Marxism—Leninism and the fact that its recruitment channel is limited to trade unions have further contributed to the JSP's inflexibility. The support that the JSP found among Japanese youth in the 1950's is not forthcoming with today's youth, and the JSP is fast becoming a party of middle-aged men, most of whom are old boys from the trade unions. As the LDP has declined, the JSP and DSP have failed to gain strength, and the Komeito and the Communist party (JCP) have increased.[15] The resulting multipolarization of Japanese politics is destined to become even more pronounced toward the second half of the 1970's.

There is, of course, the possibility that radical changes may take place. The one that comes to mind most readily is the chance that the opposition parties might form a coalition to take power. Theoretically, this would be possible if the LDP continues to decline and loses its majority in the second half of the 1970's. But barring some major adjustments in the policies and philosophies of the four opposition parties, the possibility is remote. Right now the divergence among the four opposition parties is substantial. The DSP is really a status-quo party, advocating some gradual reforms. The JSP stands on a radical platform, calling for fundamental, although "peaceful," changes in the social system and arguing for revolution but doing little to bring it about. The Komeito has strong organization and a wide variety of future courses, although it is unlikely to form an alliance with the JCP. The social backgrounds of the supporters of each party make the situation still more complicated. DSP and JSP supporters, mostly members of big industry trade unions whose standard of living has increased measurably during the 1960's, are not basically dissatisfied with present life. The JCP and Komeito followers have more grievances and frustrations, the JCP being ideological and the Komeito being more pragmatic in their solutions.

A combination of the DSP and part of the JSP is not beyond imagination, but even with Komeito it would not constitute a majority. Moreover, the JSP is split between those with ideological sympathy for the JCP and those who would prefer an alliance with the DSP and Komeito, or even a "progressive" wing of the LDP. The recent successes of the JCP have widened this split.[16] The most likely outcome of the demise of the LDP's simple majority will be confusion, a series of temporary coalitions and eventually the emergence of new political forces.

Thus Japanese politics seem to be entering a period of fluidity. If we add to the picture the recent increase in abstention, even greater fluidity is foreseeable. Abstention in Japan has risen from 23 percent in 1958 to 32 percent in 1969. One author has pointed out that the second largest political group in Japan is not those who support the JSP, but those who do not vote, a group that is almost equal to the number that vote for the LDP.[17] Many non-voters are not simply apathetic but are motivated rather by dissatisfaction with the political parties. Should new possibilities arise from the present confusion in the political scene they may change their attitude. A recent public opinion poll shows that those who support neither the LDP nor the opposition parties have increased to 30 percent of the total population.[18]

The current domestic political situation is making it difficult for policy makers to act on any front. Domestically consensus cannot be reached on the reform of Japan's economic structure. It is true that in 1972 most people in Japan agreed in theory that Japan should switch its energies to social investment to reduce the export effect of Japan's rapid economic growth and ease the unfortunate trade war. This is, in fact, one of the rationales behind Prime Minister Tanaka's plan for remodeling the Japanese Archipelago. But the plan eluded implementation: The nature of the Japanese decision-making system made it difficult to establish a focal point for the plan and financing was not forthcoming.[19] The oil crisis at the end of 1973 finally buried the idea.

The inability of the government to cope with urgent domestic problems may damage the people's confidence in the

government and further destabilize the political situation.
Signs of declining faith in the government are already apparent. (A recent poll showed that 70 percent of the people
think that the tax system is unfair although most could not
remember the amount of tax they pay.) Inherent in such a
situation is the possibility of reaction, or a sudden shift of
mood toward a demand for stronger and more positive leadership.

Thus recent developments in Japanese politics presage
change. Although it is difficult to tell the direction this
change will take, one cannot deny the possibility that a new
political force may emerge, carrying with it dramatic and
popular policies in which a nationalistic foreign policy may
be prominent. It is also likely that the LDP may take drastic
measures to rejuvenate itself, particularly in the field of
domestic policy. The effect of such change would probably
be beneficial. However, these drastic measures may also bear
on foreign policy, using popular nationalistic appeals. Unfortunately, most governments find it easier to take initiatives in
the field of foreign policy.

IMPLICATIONS FOR U.S.-JAPANESE RELATIONS

The most obvious target of a foreign policy shift in Japan
would be the Security Treaty. It is not unthinkable that the
LDP will try to revise the treaty or even to terminate it. The
LDP's continuous advocacy of the Security Treaty has made
it difficult for the party to capitalize on growing nationalistic
sentiment, and the LDP leadership may decide eventually
that the treaty has become a political liability. Such a decision, however, is unlikely for at least three or four years,
because many Japanese still feel that the treaty is important
for Japan. Furthermore, the U.S.-Japanese security alliance
now enjoys wide international acceptance. Both China and

the Soviet Union probably view the treaty as a means of assuring that Japan will not fall under the other's sphere of influence. There can be little doubt that termination of the treaty would make Chinese and Soviet leaders uneasy and heighten the tension between the two countries. Any Japanese government cannot help but feel the influence of this prospect. Also, the declining tension in Asia in general—recognizing that several local spots of tension remain—can nevertheless be said to have eased the difficulty of managing the alliance because the opposition can no longer argue that the treaty is likely to involve Japan in conflict.

In the near future, the more likely prospect for U.S.-Japanese security relations will be a gradual reduction of the American military presence in Japan, a course that would appeal most directly to the domestic political situation in both countries. Nevertheless, this will inevitably raise the question of the credibility of the mutual security commitment. While it is important that Japan assume a more responsible attitude toward defense problems (not necessarily by increasing the defense budget), if greater responsibility leads to a lesser degree of cooperation with the United States, Japan's security position will weaken and possibly destabilize the situation in Northeast Asia. Unless the two governments are imaginative and farsighted, there may only be a reduction of American forces in Japan without any system to replace them.

Economic relations between Japan and the United States are in some ways more difficult and in other ways easier to handle. On the one hand, minor conflicts are likely to arise frequently because both countries are entering a period of change in industrial structure that will be a difficult and painful process. With continued weak leadership in Japan, the necessary adjustment measures will probably come belatedly. External influence, especially American demands for liberalization in trade and capital investment or for adjustments in trade agreements, will be resisted strongly in Japan. On the other hand, the Japanese, at least theoretically, realize the necessity of mutual interdependence. In Japan it is easier to argue for closer and more equitable economic relations with the United States than it is to make the case for security ties. In this sense, Japan's performance since 1971 demonstrates that it tends to be more responsive to economic pressures. But finesse and imagination are still required. Though it can be argued that the second "Nixon shock" had the beneficial effect of making the Japanese act, the cumulative effect of such shocks must not be neglected. Beyond a certain point they can result in reaction. Also, the measures that must be taken to improve mutual economic relations, while beneficial to both economies in the long run, will hurt particular industries in the short run. As in the case of textiles, these industries may attempt to politicize their problems in order to enlist wider support to resist the measures being taken against them.

Thus it seems fundamentally important for Japan and the United States to concentrate on the constructive and positive elements in their relations with each other. Cooperative measures toward further detente in Asia are one such possibility, joint efforts toward the evolution of a new international economic order are another. The Security Treaty may continue to exist out of sheer necessity and the two countries may manage somehow to avoid a serious clash of economic interests. However, if the relation is to be based upon nothing but necessity, the future can only be bleak. Unless it is strengthened by some positive sense of a common goal, it lacks real meaning. And in order to develop such a sense, efforts on the part of the Japanese to assert themselves constructively seem essential.

3

PRISCILLA CLAPP

U.S. Domestic Politics
and Relations with Japan

Events of the last decade have impressed on American observers the vital relationship between domestic politics and the conduct of foreign policy. Not only is a nation's foreign policy shaped by factors within the domestic body politic, but its foreign policy must respond, at least in general, to the aspirations, values, and mood of the society it serves. The foreign policy of a government democratically elected evolves from a process of pulling and a hauling among competing forces within the government and the society, more than it does from the demands of the outside world.

There can be little doubt that the American political system has undergone unprecedented strain in the last few years, calling into question the credibility of both elected and appointed officials, the wisdom of what were once commonly accepted principles of U.S. conduct in the world, and the capability of the political system itself to cope effectively with modern problems. Almost the entire American population has in one way or another been touched by the debate and the problems underlying it. The dramatic shift toward national self-reflection is already beginning to find expression in basic public attitudes toward what is acceptable and what is not acceptable in U.S. foreign policy, in challenges to formerly unchallenged authority for the conduct of that foreign policy, and in the relative weight of competing groups within the government bureaucracy for leadership on foreign policy matters.

In this chapter I will examine changing patterns of opinion and influence in the United States as they relate to foreign policy in general and Japan in particular. Five major categories of influence in policy making will be treated: public opinion, the press, the Congress, the bureaucracy, and the presidency. Finally, an attempt will be made to draw some general conclusions about the constraints, problems, and opportunities these changes will present to U.S.-Japanese relations.

PUBLIC OPINION

During the decade of the 1960's the factor of public opinion or the "public mood" gained significant weight in the policy-making process in large part as a result of recognition within the U.S. government that involvement in Vietnam was seriously undermining public confidence in the American leadership. For the first time since World War II, public opinion turned against the theory that the executive branch—particularly the office of the President—should enjoy a relatively free hand to decide and pursue U.S. foreign policy. Although it can hardly be said that the experience of Vietnam has brought about a permanent public interest in foreign policy matters, it has served to ensure that in the foreseeable future U.S. policy makers will not operate under the axiom that public consensus will automatically support the President's judgment on foreign policy.

Since 1965 we have witnessed a shift in public consensus not only on the extent to which U.S. commitments abroad are acceptable but also on the importance of foreign versus domestic concerns. A public opinion survey in 1964 revealed that Americans rated the six most important national concerns as:

1. keeping the country out of war;
2. combatting world communism;
3. keeping our military defense strong;
4. controlling the use of nuclear weapons;
5. maintaining respect for the United States in other countries;
6. maintaining law and order.

By mid-1972 only one item of foreign policy remained among the top six on the list of national concerns, which read as follows:

1. rising prices and the cost of living;
2. the amount of violence in American life;
3. the problem of drug addicts and narcotic drugs;
4. crime in this country;
5. the problem of Vietnam;
6. cleaning up our waterways and reducing water pollution.[1]

The dramatic decline in the national fear of communism has been accompanied by a public desire for greater restraint in the use of force. The public majority in 1964 that agreed it would be worthwhile for the United States to go to war to preserve its position of power had disappeared by 1972. Furthermore, there was strong public endorsement of President Nixon's efforts to bring about new understandings with China and the Soviet Union. Even after the Strategic Arms Limitation agreement was signed in Moscow in 1972, 80 percent of the American public felt that the United States should negotiate further arms reductions with the Soviet Union.

In spite of the obvious shift of public priorities toward domestic concerns, opinion polls have not revealed a strongly isolationist trend in the public mood. A majority still supports U.S. cooperation in the United Nations, consultation with allies on foreign policy decisions, and consideration of the needs of other countries when making U.S. foreign policy. Finally, it should be noted that, while the trend in public thinking on foreign policy has been toward restraint in U.S. actions abroad, a distinct majority still feels that the threat of conflict in the world has not abated.

If these are the general inclinations of American public thinking on general questions of foreign policy in the wake of the disturbing Vietnam experience, it is much more difficult to establish a definite public mood with regard to Japan. The two major factors of public thinking that emerge from opinion polls directed specifically at Japan are: that the American public is generally disinterested and uninformed about Japan; and that a strong majority favors a close relationship with Japan.

On the issue of security relations, a poll taken by the *Asahi* newspaper in 1971 found that only 39 percent of those Americans polled were aware of the U.S.-Japan Mutual Security Treaty.[2] When informed of the treaty some 68 percent replied that it represented a U.S. obligation to help if Japan were attacked by another nation, while 74 percent assumed that it also implied an obligation on the part of Japan to help the United States in a major war in the vicinity of Japan. A mid-1972 poll revealed that 43 percent of the American public would advise that the United States should come to the defense of Japan with military force (compared with a slightly higher 52 percent for Western Europe.)[3] The *Asahi* poll mentioned above and a similar poll by the *Yomiuri* newspaper in 1971 reflected a majority opinion in the United States against a Japanese military build-up, particularly in nuclear weapons.[4]

There appears to be an increasing ambivalence in American opinion toward Japan vis-à-vis China. Gallup polls taken in

1972 and 1973 indicate that, although a majority felt both countries were a stabilizing force in Asia, Japan had the larger majority in 1972 and China had the larger majority in 1973.[5] Similarly, during the same one-year span, the majority who earlier felt that Japan was the best partner for securing U.S. interests in Asia had swung to China by 1973. Undoubtedly, this fluctuation was more closely related to the public exuberance over the thaw in U.S.-China relations than to any particular disenchantment with Japan.

Signs of ambivalence and contradiction can also be found in American public opinion about economic relations between Japan and the United States. The *Asahi* and *Yomiuri* polls of 1971 found that some 50 to 70 percent of the respondents felt that the United States was threatened by Japanese economic advances. However, Gallup polls conducted in March 1972 and 1973 demonstrated that only 28 and 34 percent, respectively, of those polled felt that Japan was an economic threat to the United States, while 59 percent and 52 percent, respectively, felt that Japanese economic strength was an asset to the United States. The later polls also reflected that a large majority was in favor of increasing the volume of U.S.-Japanese trade.

The general American image of the Japanese has improved gradually over the postwar period. Between 1942 and 1966, descriptive adjectives such as "intelligent" and "progressive" drew increasingly more positive responses than those like "sly," "warlike," and "radical." Whereas some 63 percent of Americans polled in 1942 described the Japanese as sly, only 19 percent used the same description in 1966. That some 20 to 25 percent of the American public will continue to believe that the Japanese people are sly is not without significance, however. In reporting on its American poll of 1971, the *Asahi Evening News* featured the fact that one in four respondents felt that "Orientals, including the Japanese, are sly

and devious—we should never trust or rely on them as allies."
These residual misgivings about the Japanese among the
American public are easily stimulated when the media indi-
cates a sense of conflict in the relationship.

It is probably true that the great majority of Americans has
no clear sense of what policy toward Japan should be and
that, as in most specific issues of foreign policy, they will
generally fall into line when official policy is clarified and
publicized. A Harris poll taken in December 1969, just after
President Nixon and Prime Minister Sato had reached agreement on return of Okinawa to Japan, asked the question,
"Do you feel that the United States should give Okinawa
back to the Japanese or not." Fifty percent replied *no,* 26
percent replied *yes,* and 24 percent had no opinion. Yet there
was virtually no public reaction two years later when the
treaty for the return of Okinawa was concluded.

Undoubtedly more influential on U.S. policy toward Japan
are the pressure groups representing special interests for the
public. Those like the American Legion and the Veterans of
Foreign Wars, tend to advocate a larger security role for
Japan and to support the broader interests of the U.S. military in Asia. Presumably they would try to rally public
support on issues where the American military indicated a
special interest.

In the late 1960's and early 1970's labor and business
leaders became particularly vocal, calling both public and
official attention to the threat that Japanese products pose to
certain sectors of American industry. The most glaring example of this kind of pressure occurred with regard to Japanese
textile exports to the United States. When Richard Nixon
was running for President in 1968, he felt that the only way
to win the presidential nomination from the Republican
party was to secure the votes of Strom Thurmond and the
other Southern delegates at the convention. In return for his

support, Thurmond, among other things, exacted a promise from Nixon that he would champion quota protection for the U.S. textile industry. After he won the nomination, Nixon met with the textile industry leaders and gave them an effective veto over U.S. trade policy toward Japan once he became President.[6]

THE PRESS

American newspapers devote very little space to foreign affairs. What does get into print must compete with everything else to get only two and a third minutes of attention a day from the average reader.[7] Reporters and editors must select foreign affairs news that will attract the attention of a generally disinterested public or that will appeal to a foreign policy elite consisting mostly of government officials. Naturally, those items which stress conflict tend to get the most play, and conflict tends to be stressed where it may be only marginally present.

A careful observer of the American foreign policy press corps has judged that most of these reporters tend toward a liberal internationalist position in their policy preferences. They favor U.S. involvement in world affairs and international institutions, they endorse liberal trade policies, and they support American institutions in the face of foreign, particularly Soviet, challenge.[8] Washington reporters are inclined to cater to an elite readership that takes an active and consistent interest in foreign policy, namely, government officials, members of Congress and a small interested public. Often they consciously report to one part of the government what another part is doing.

Like the public, the American press was, until the late 1960's, inclined to defer to the wisdom of the President on foreign policy matters. Most Washington reporters accepted the role of explaining to the public the logic behind U.S. foreign policy actions, particularly when the explanations came from high sources, and they provided a means of communication within government. In many cases, it was the press who elevated executive pronouncements to the level of doctrine.

The experience with Vietnam has probably ensured that there will not be a return to that mentality during the lifetime of the current press corps. Since 1967, perhaps even earlier, there has been a marked tendency among Washington reporters covering foreign policy matters to question executive policy and actions and to point out the inconsistencies or conflicts between competing parts of the government bureaucracy. In some ways it might be said that the press is now making, as well as reporting, the news. It was the press that found and publicized the duplicity in the Nixon administration's explanation of the 1972 Watergate break-in, eventually bringing the office of the President to task on a range of issues including excesses in the name of national security—a hitherto sacrosanct sphere of executive activity. In late 1973 the Washington press corps raised unprecedented questions about the motivations of the President and Secretary of State in calling a national military alert during the Middle East war. This was not only a caution against precipitous commitment of U.S. troops abroad. Ten years ago it would have been unthinkable to suggest publicly that the President might have been acting out of personal interest rather than national interest by alerting U.S. forces.

If foreign affairs in general tend to occupy a modest portion of the American news, reporting on Japan is miniscule. This was particularly apparent during the 1960's when there were few issues of contention between Japan and the United States. Furthermore, policy was largely in the hands of the Japan experts in the bureaucracy and contentious issues tended to be removed in both form and substance from the public view. Articles on Japan during this decade largely reflected the conflict in social change in Japan, political suicides, signs of Japanese militarism, violent student demonstrations, and so on.

Since the beginning of the 1970's, however, there has been a notable change in both volume and content of reporting on Japan in major American newspapers. The number of articles on Japan in the *New York Times,* generally considered the most sophisticated national newspaper on foreign policy issues, increased by 20 percent between 1970 and 1972 and, naturally, began to occupy a more prominent position in the paper.[9] On the negative side, during the same two-year period the substance of articles and editorials, particularly those of weekly news magazines, were instrumental in promoting images of intricately coordinated government—business collusion in Japan, unbeatable Japanese economic competition, rampant Japanese "workoholism"—in short, the "economic animal."[10] It is also interesting that the great majority of articles on Japan in weekly magazines now deals with economic conditions, commerce, and industry.

On the positive side, reporting of political developments in Japan, U.S.-Japanese diplomacy, and Japanese reactions to U.S. policy in major newspapers has been broader and more balanced. Of course, it should also be taken into account that the early 1970's has seen a remarkable increase in high-level government contacts between the United States and Japan, conditioned no doubt by recognition of Japan's emergence as a large power, as well as by a series of economic and diplomatic problems.

Nevertheless, coverage of Japan in the general American press is still very uneven and given to the exotic. While it is true that the wire services (AP and UPI) tend to produce a balanced array of articles on Japan, those that get published are chosen at the discretion of local U.S. editors who seem to favor stories perpetuating or conforming to old images of Japan.[11] Only the larger U.S. newspapers devote any substantial space to interpretive news on social and political trends in Japan. Because Japan still ranks behind the Soviet Union, England, France, Germany, and Israel in relative degree of coverage, stories on Japan that don't carry eyecatching headlines face stiff competition for space.

There are two basic implications here for U.S.-Japanese relations. First, the American press is now much more likely to challenge executive policy. This has already been evident in the adverse reaction of some reporters and editorial writers to the attitudes in the White House that led to the "Nixon shocks." Second, the interested elite gets little basic information on Japan from the American press and probably tends to see more conflict in the relationship than there actually is because those articles that are published more often than not stress such conflict.

THE CONGRESS

During most of the postwar period, Congress has deferred to the notion that the legislative branch should confine its influence to the domestic sphere and leave foreign policy more or less to the initiative of the executive branch. Until recently militant anti-communism and a strong military posture found little opposition in Congress. Conservatives, although hesitant for the United States to become involved in foreign conflict, supported U.S. involvement once a commitment had been made. Liberals stood behind President John F. Kennedy's inaugural incantations to "pay any price, bear any burden, meet any hardship, support any friend, oppose any foe, in order to assure the survival and the success of liberty." During the 1960's, however, particularly after 1965, changes that were occurring in the composition and attitudes of Congress began to manifest themselves in executive-legislative relations in the area of foreign policy. Vietnam, of course, was the catalyst.

In composition, the Senate, while it has traditionally been somewhat more likely to question executive authority than the House, began to shift decisively toward a critical stance, taking issue with almost the entire foreign policy of the executive branch: U.S. involvement in Vietnam, U.S. policy toward Communist China, U.S. military spending, the maintenance of large U.S. military bases overseas, foreign assistance and military aid, and so on. The more moderate to liberal composition of the Senate—and the House to a lesser extent—has not only resulted from new elections; a number of older members in positions of seniority have changed their colors.

Even more important, lines between conservative and liberal philosophies on foreign policy have blurred and, in some instances, reversed. What might have been hypothetical in earlier arguments for and against U.S. involvement abroad became very real in the context of Vietnam. Neither liberal nor conservative was happy with the way the executive branch was handling the war in Vietnam. Both began to lean toward a reduction of U.S. commitments and involvements abroad.[12]

Thus since 1965 Congressional attempts to limit or modify the foreign policy of the executive branch have become much more frequent. The most notable efforts in recent years have involved questions of legislative control over executive authority to commit U.S. forces abroad. In 1969 the Senate stipulated that no funds in the defense appropriations bill be used to finance "the introduction of American ground combat troops into Laos or Thailand;" in 1970 the Senate passed an amendment to restrict U.S. military operations in Cambodia; and in 1973 both the Senate and House voted to cut off funds for further U.S. bombing in Southeast Asia. Simultaneous to these more ad hoc and ex post facto shots at controlling executive actions through fund cut-offs, a separate effort was underway to redefine the responsibility of Congress in granting authority *ab initio* for the President to commit U.S. forces to combat. At the initiative of Senator Javits, Congress succeeded in drawing up a War Powers Bill to prohibit the President from ordering U.S. troops into combat abroad for longer than 60 days without the approval of both Houses. In 1973 the bill was enacted into law by Congress over the President's veto.

On matters of military funding Congress has also begun to impose controls, where earlier in the 1960's it might have been inclined to vote larger appropriations than were actually requested. Although the House still maintains a stand on military spending that is basically in favor of the Pentagon, the Senate has succeeded in demanding a series of funding cuts since 1969.[13] It should be noted that no major new weapons system has ever been defeated on the floor in Congress.[14] It is probably not misrepresentative to say, however, that the ABM debate in Congress in 1971 had the effect of bringing opposing scientific opinion to bear on the question, forcing military leaders and administration officials to back away from their claims supporting extensive ABM deployments.

Obviously the executive branch has not, on the whole, appreciated these manifestations of Congressional prerogative on questions of national security and foreign policy. The relationship between the executive and legislative branches became especially antagonistic in the early 1970's, a situation that the White House itself promoted until the events surrounding the Watergate scandal began to take their toll on the President. However, since Henry Kissinger has been Secretary of State, he has been careful to consult frequently with the Senate Foreign Relations Committee, in part to reverse the trend of mounting antagonism at least in the field of foreign policy.[15]

During the postwar period Japan has never loomed very large on the Congressional horizon, although interest in U.S.-Japanese relations has begun to receive somewhat increased attention in this forum in recent years. During the 1950's and 1960's the issues most frequently, albeit sporadically, aired on the floor of the House or Senate related to trade and particularly textiles. For a brief period in 1960 there was considerable debate in both houses about the riots in Japan over the revised security treaty and the resultant cancellation of President Eisenhower's visit to Japan. While there have been a number of hearings over the years on treaty commitments with Japan, U.S. policy in Asia, and aid appropriations to Okinawa, they have been perfunctory in the sense that they mounted no effective challenges to executive policy.

What effect Congress may have had on the executive branch approach to U.S.-Japanese relations during the 1960's was more indirect. For example, in 1967 Senator Richard Russell, chairman of the Senate Armed Services Committee, informally vetoed language that the executive branch proposed entering into the Johnson—Sato joint communique (November 1967) to indicate that the American government intended to return the administrative rights over Okinawa to Japan in the foreseeable future. President Johnson, sensitive to the possibility of an adverse reaction among Congressional conservatives to the return of Okinawa to Japan, whereby they might successfully block a treaty, deferred to Senator Russell's advice, and the final decision on reversion was put off two years. By 1971, when the treaty on Okinawa reversion finally came to the Senate for ratification, the specter of a conservative reaction which the executive branch had anticipated, never did emerge.[16]

Between 1969 and 1971 Representative Wilbur Mills, chairman of the House Ways and Means Committee, became heavily involved in efforts under way to gain a voluntary textile quota agreement with the Japanese government. Although he was a free trader by nature, he consistently and frequently threatened legislated textile quotas in order to make the executive branch's case for the less restrictive voluntary quotas more convincing to the Japanese. Later, in 1971, Mills negotiated directly with representatives of the Japanese textile industry seeking to arrange their unilateral restraint as a means of avoiding legislated quotas.

The most direct threat of legislative action in Congress that would affect U.S. relations with Japan occurred in connection with the strongly protectionist Burke-Hartke Bill, recommending severe restrictions on Japanese imports to the United States. However, the bill was never reported out of the House Ways and Means Committee and none of its protectionist provisions were incorporated in the Trade Reform Act, which passed the House in 1973.

One might characterize the dominant attitude in Congress toward Japan as benevolent and somewhat patronizing, but there do appear to be residuals of mistrust important enough to cause some concern. The majority of the members of both Houses, of course, have been conditioned by the experience of World War II and have had little if any direct experience with Japan since then.[17] As long as the U.S. relations with Japan are smooth, it would be difficult to identify, much less measure, any latent feeling in Congress against a strong and even intimate U.S.-Japanese relationship. There is also a significant number of Congressmen and Senators who will speak out against what they consider to be potentially unfair policies toward Japan. However, should Japanese actions appear to be the cause of any problems in U.S.-Japanese relations, feelings of hostility within Congress tend to come to the surface. This was most recently apparent in the years between 1969 and 1972 when a significant contingent within Congress, backed by organized labor and select industry leaders, was trying to legislate restrictions on imports to the United States. Although any restrictions legislated by Congress would affect most of the countries that export to the United States, there is little doubt that Japanese imports were viewed as the most serious threat. With the Arab oil embargo of late 1973, Congressional concern shifted away from trade problems with the industrialized countries and toward the problem of assuring raw material supplies. It is likely that for the foreseeable future, this will remain a dominant concern of Congress and there will be a tendency to identify more with Japan in terms of trade problems that both countries have in common.

On security issues Japanese actions have never given Congress reason for significant concern. When the administrative rights over Okinawa were returned to Japan, it was clearly explained by the executive branch that, although the move was largely a response to political pressures in Japan, it was being done by the U.S. government as a tribute to good relations with Japan and would not cause any appreciable deterioration in the U.S. strategic position in the Far East. It is possible that had the executive branch—or even a few top military leaders—portrayed to Congress a situation in which the Japanese were demanding the return of Okinawa with threats against U.S.-Japanese relations, there would have been an extreme reaction in Congress against Japan and there would have been little hope for reaching an amicable agreement on the return of Okinawa. There is always the chance that precipitous action by the Japanese government to abrogate the security treaty would arouse the wrath of Congress, because Congress in general would have little basis for understanding the political situation in Japan that would lead to such an event. One must assume, however, that the foreign policy experts and diplomats in both governments would take all possible steps to avoid any such abrupt change in bilateral relations.

THE BUREAUCRACY

Until the mid-1960's it was axiomatic among those in the U.S. government bureaucracy who dealt with foreign affairs and national security that: the world was divided into two distinct groupings—non-Communist and Communist, good and bad; the Communist world, directed by Moscow or Peking, was expansionist with unlimited objectives for taking over the world; and the United States was responsible for the leadership and strength of the free world to resist Communist takeover. Anti-Communist militancy thus placed strong priorities on military power. It further indicated that the United States should gain and secure as many allies as possible for the non-Communist camp.

As public debate over Vietnam and other questions began to mount in the late 1960's, groups and individuals within the bureaucracy, who might earlier have questioned the premises of blind anti-communism but remained silent, began to speak out. In short, the result has been a decline in the power and position of the military within the bureaucratic bargaining process. Naturally, the new inclination of Congress to scrutinize and question military spending and programs has also contributed greatly to the decline in bureaucratic power of the military.

In the area of national security and international relations the weight lost by the military has inevitably shifted toward civilian officials in the Pentagon, the White House, and to a lesser extent the State Department. Even more important, however, has been the recent shift of emphasis in foreign relations toward economic problems. This has predictably tended to increase the role of those bureaucrats with expertise in economic affairs, both domestic and international. The great concern with energy and raw material supplies should ensure them a prominent position in foreign policy making over the next decade.

These shifts in power and attitudes within the bureaucracy have already had some very important effects on U.S.-Japanese relations, in both security and economic matters. The debate within the U.S. bureaucracy that resulted in the decision to return Okinawa to Japan occurred against a background of growing disenchantment with the American role in Vietnam. In 1966, when the relevant parts of the bureaucracy[18] embarked on the task of reviewing and defining the status of the U.S. presence in Okinawa and the pressures against that presence, military requirements for maintaining control over Okinawa had not been effectively challenged since the end of the war. If there hadn't been, within the bureaucracy, serious questions about the U.S. role in Vietnam and the reality of the Chinese threat, if there hadn't been a general reaction against unnecessary military spending and a shift away from large overseas bases, the case being made by civilian bureaucrats for the need to return Okinawa to preserve harmonious U.S.-Japanese relations would not have made much progress against military resistance. If the Joint Chiefs of Staff hadn't already lost some important battles with civilian analysts in areas where military judgments had formerly reigned supreme, they probably would have felt more inclined to stick to their guns on Okinawa, mustering public support through Congress.

It would be difficult to imagine the appearance in the

1970's of a situation in U.S.-Japanese security relations where military leaders within the U.S. bureaucracy could hold the amount of control over U.S. decision making as they did in the 1950's and 1960's with regard to the administration of Okinawa. In the area of economic and trade relations, however, there may be more reason for concern that forces within the U.S. bureaucracy who are responding almost exclusively to domestic political and personal interests could push U.S. decision making in directions detrimental to U.S.-Japanese relations.

The competing forces within the bureaucracy on economic issues are numerous. The Commerce and Agriculture Departments are involved in trade issues. Commerce, in particular, tends to represent protectionist interests. The Treasury Department is concerned with international monetary issues, the balance of payments, and, to an extent, trade—although not from a protectionist point of view. The State Department becomes involved in all trade and economic matters, usually with a view toward keeping these issues in balance diplomatically. There is also a Special Trade Representative to handle international negotiations. Within the White House there tend to be two warring factions: the protectionist voices raised by presidential aides who are concerned with political pay-offs to industries or groups who have made campaign contributions, and the more liberal voices within the National Security Council staff and the Council on International Economic Policy. Which of these forces gains control of a particular issue can determine how the issue is handled. If the State Department is forced out of an effective role in the process, decision makers can lose sight of the interplay between the issue at hand and other issues in a bilateral relation.

In the dispute between the United States and Japan over textile quotas, it became only too clear that powerful nationalist and protectionist pressures could be brought to bear on the foreign policy process within the bureaucracy to force decisions contrary to amicable relations between the two countries. Through a series of narrow political considerations, related and unrelated,[19] President Nixon entrusted the solution of the textile problem to individuals within the U.S. bureaucracy whose interests tended to be parochial and whose experience with foreign affairs and particularly U.S.-Japanese relations was almost nonexistent. Once the responsibility for textiles was lodged in the hands of an old Nixon loyalist like Secretary of Commerce Maurice Stans and it was understood that the President wanted an expeditious solution to repay a political debt, it was very difficult for more moderate forces within the bureaucracy, even Henry Kissinger, to challenge that authority without risking attack from the entire contingent of powerful Nixon loyalists.

Undoubtedly, the problem lies as much in the nature of the issue as in the process. Economic issues are more likely to have identifiable domestic constituencies and clear domestic consequences than are international political, and even security, matters. When these domestic constituencies are well organized, the pressure they can bring to bear on decision makers, especially those whose power runs directly from the President, can be important to the way the issue is presented to the other country or countries involved.

THE PRESIDENT

All these groups I have been discussing thus far look ultimately to the President for direction in American foreign policy. The office of the President provides important linkage between domestic interests and diplomacy. How he restructures bureaucratic machinery or uses the existing structure and to whom he entrusts primary responsibility for accomplishing his foreign policy objectives have a great deal of influence on the outcome of the decision making process.

Foreign policy has been of vital concern to Richard Nixon during his presidency and he has taken measures to ensure that he can gain as much control as possible over major decisions. Needless to say, he has found a powerful instrument to this end in Henry Kissinger, Secretary of State and Assistant to the President for National Security Affairs. Together they have compiled a commendable record of foreign policy achievements and must be given fair credit for having plunged into major problems of diplomacy and come out ahead: strategic arms limitations with the Soviet Union, normalization of U.S. relations with Communist China, U.S. withdrawal from Vietnam, controlling conflict in the Middle East.

Japan, however, has not been one of their strong points. Although President Nixon came to office with a better awareness of Japan than any postwar U.S. President, he has wavered between the traditional wisdom of maintaining a strong alliance with Japan and domestic pressures for economic protection. Even as he was reaching successful conclusion of an agreement with Japan to return the administrative rights over Okinawa, he was promoting a highly protectionist move toward the limitation of Japanese textile exports to the United States. Before the success of Okinawa reversion could even be counted, the relationship was being rocked by the textile dispute. Japan's failure to act quickly on the textile issue according to the President's wishes[20] undoubtedly contributed substantially to the presidential attitude toward Japan that later manifested itself in the "Nixon shocks." Although the psychological effects of the shocks in Japan may have been far greater than the White House anticipated, they were evidently calculated to nudge Japan away from what was perceived as a client relationship with the United States.

In his 1973 foreign policy message, the President described his policy toward Japan as follows:

The intimacy of the postwar U.S.-Japanese alliance, . . . inevitably gave Japan a special sensitivity to the evolution of United States foreign policy. We thus found the paradox that Japan seemed to feel that her reliance on us should limit change or initiative in American policy, even while she was actively seeking new directions in many dimensions of her own policy. But our abandoning our paternalistic style of alliance leadership meant not that we were casting Japan or any ally adrift, but that we took our allies more seriously, as full partners. Our recognizing the new multipolarity of the world meant not a loss of interest in our alliances, but the contrary—an acknowledgement of the new importance of our allies. American initiatives, such as in China policy or economic policy were not directed against Japan, but were taken in a common interest or in a much broader context.

Whatever the intention, the result has been to focus Japanese attention on White House attitudes and actions. The strength and breadth of common interests between the two countries becomes overshadowed by the personalized diplomacy of Henry Kissinger and obsession with defining his true intentions toward Japan. The apparent efforts of President Nixon and Henry Kissinger to break the umbilical cord between the United States and Japan have reinforced the suspicion in Japan that the President and Secretary of State are really only interested in nuclear power balances. No matter what they say to the contrary, this impression now has a life of its own.

CONCLUSIONS

Several general and specific conclusions are suggested by this admittedly cursory review of changing conditions in the U.S. domestic scene:

1. In the future, the American public will be more concerned with domestic problems and foreign policy as it relates to or affects domestic problems, rather than with the

ideological aspects of foreign policy. This does not mean that the public will turn abruptly isolationist. It was most interesting during the recent Arab oil embargo that the American public tended to focus its hostility on the American oil companies, not on the Arab countries. The notion of reprisals against the Arabs never gained any wide popularity in the United States.

2. The American press, for the foreseeable future, will maintain a more skeptical view of the government's foreign policy. Although the press can be expected to continue to look for easy or clever explanations for phenomena such as rapid Japanese economic growth, it also has great potential for improving American understanding of Japan. As American reporters become more experienced in reporting on Japan (as I believe to be inevitable), they should develop the capacity to bring more effective criticism to bear on U.S. actions or potential actions that disregard the interests of good relations between the United States and Japan.

3. Congressional influence on foreign policy will be stronger in the 1970's than it has been in the past twenty years. Whether this influence will always be directed toward constructive objectives is not predictable. Congress can be expected to sustain pressure on the executive branch to reduce military bases and commitments abroad. Attitudes in Congress toward Japan are bound to become somewhat more stable as staff expertise on foreign affairs improves. However, there will always be a substantial number of congressmen and senators with no intrinsic interest in foreign relations or Japan, who can be expected to respond primarily to nationalistic stimuli. This is a fact of life that Japanese policy makers must include in their calculations as a constant.

4. The interest among the public, the press, and the Congress in questioning foreign and national security policy has increased dramatically. Not only will this place restraints on

executive actions, it may also provide the impetus for the executive branch to move in new directions, as it has with regard to detente and China policy.

5. The battle between the protectionists and free traders will continue to be issue oriented. The success of the protectionists will depend on the public base of support and the locus of power within the bureaucracy. To the extent that the consumer is organizing an interest group and that inflation is serious, the protectionists will find it more difficult to make their case for trade barriers.

6. As Japan's role in international affairs increases during the 1970's, its visibility in the United States will also increase. This could have two significant effects. First, as Americans become accustomed to thinking of Japan as a powerful international actor, there may be new expectations for Japanese support of U.S. policies in return for the years that the United States assisted Japan. Much depends on how well Japan's position is explained, particularly to Congress. Second, Japan's increased visibility in the United States will, in a sense, give Japan less freedom of action just at the time when it is becoming more active internationally. With more attention focused on Japan than there has been in the past, the chances will be greater for critical scrutiny of Japanese foreign policy in general.

4

HISAO KANAMORI

Future U.S.-Japanese
Economic Relations

The volume of trade between the United States and Japan indicates that the relationship between the two economies is close. In 1970 total trade between the two countries surpassed $10 billion; it increased to $19 billion in 1973. The only other bilateral trade relationship that has ever exceeded $10 billion in value is that between the United States and Canada.

Basically, there are two reasons why U.S.-Japanese trade has taken on such massive proportions. First, both countries have extremely large economies; the United States has the largest GNP in the world, and Japan ranks second in the free world. Second, there is a kind of economic complementarity between the two countries. While the United States is endowed with highly advanced technological capability and vast natural resources, Japan has a medium technological capability, a relatively cheap labor force, and very few natural resources. Therefore, the United States imports from Japan commodities that require medium technology and intensive labor, and Japan imports from the United States high technology and raw materials.

The. U.S.-Japanese trade structure can be more tangibly

expressed by grouping Japan's export commodities in two large categories: medium technology industrial products, such as automobiles, radios, television sets, portable electronic calculators, iron, steel, and so on; labor-intensive industrial products, such as clothing, footwear, veneer, toys, and so on. (Table 1 in the appendix to this chapter represents a breakdown of the commodity trade between the United States and Japan.)

Similarly, Japan's major import commodities can be classified broadly as: agricultural products, such as soy beans, wheat, corn; raw materials, such as lumber, coal, iron ore; high technology industrial products such as aircraft, electronic computers, metal-processing machinery. Until quite recently trade relations between the two nations have been developing favorably along these lines, with only occasional friction where certain marginal U.S. industries were being directly threatened by the import of cheap Japanese commodities.

THE CONFLICT IN U.S.-JAPANESE TRADE

In the latter half of the 1960's, the relatively smooth and peaceful development of trade between the United States and Japan began to dissipate (see Tables 2 and 3 in the appendix). There were two simultaneous phases to this collapse. Phase one took the form of an imbalance in commodity trade. In about 1965 Japanese exports to the United States began to exceed imports, increasing continuously to an export surplus that registered $3.8 billion in 1972. The second phase was characterized by a sharp increase in Japanese exports to the United States, while U.S. exports to Japan remained fairly constant. Japanese exports to the United States increased from 7 percent of total U.S. imports in 1960 to 16 percent of the total in 1970. At the same time, U.S. exports to Japan only increased from 8 percent to 11 percent of total Japanese imports. This sharp increase in Japanese imports in the United States triggered a reaction by many threatened U.S. industries, such as cotton fabrics, ceramics, iron and steel, seeking to restrict these imports.

Thus the U.S.-Japanese trade relationship turned from one of harmony to one of disharmony. There seem to have been three basic factors at the root of these imbalances, all relating directly or indirectly to certain characteristics of the domestic economies of the two countries.

First, there were important differences in trade structure. Most of the commodities exported by Japan to the United States enjoyed high income elasticity. In other words, they tended to be luxury consumer items the demand for which was rising faster than the average income of those buying them. Furthermore, during the rapid development of the Japanese economy in the 1960's the relative economic weight of these commodities also increased. The Japanese production of consumer goods rose to meet the greater demands of the American market. On the other hand, the raw materials that Japan imports from the United States have low income elasticity.

Thus some economists (H. S. Houthakker and S. P. Mages) have observed that when the U.S. real income increases by one percent, Japan's real exports to the United States increase by 3.5 percent. At the same time, when Japan's real income increases by one percent, U.S. exports to Japan do not increase by more than 1.1 percent. As a result, the rate of increase of Japanese exports to the United States exceeds the rate of increase of Japanese imports from the United States.

Second, Japan's ability to produce competitive exports was stimulated by rising prices (inflation) in the United States. Meanwhile, inflation in the Japanese economy was still low enough that Japan's export prices could remain stable. For example, while U.S. wholesale prices rose 16 percent between 1960 and 1970 Japan's export prices rose no more than 6 percent. (Japan's export prices have, of course, risen at a greater rate since 1971.)

Finally, U.S. exports to Japan were hampered by Japanese import restrictions. To protect its own agriculture and infant industries, the Japanese government had imposed heavy restrictions on imports.

Obviously, both governments came to recognize that these trends could not be allowed to continue through the 1970's. If the rates of increase of GNP, exports, imports, and so on, that pertained in 1971 were projected without adjustment, the Japanese trade surplus with the United States could have been expected to reach $18 billion in 1980, and Japanese goods would then constitute 32 percent of total U.S. imports (see Table 3). U.S. leaders did not feel that their economy was capable of coping with such large trade imbalances and between 1971 and 1973 the Japanese government took a series of measures to reverse the trend toward greater imbalance, namely the adjustment of exchange rates and the liberalization of trade and capital movement. By the end of 1973, the Japanese trade surplus with the United States had decreased dramatically. For economic relations between the two countries to continue to develop harmoniously in the future, careful attention must be given by both governments to maintain the conditions that will prevent such major disharmonies from arising.

CONDITIONS FOR AVOIDING IMBALANCE

If conditions can be created between two countries (or even among groups of countries) to reverse trends toward trade disharmonies, what are they and how extensive must they be? There appear to be nine basic approaches to solving such problems.

1. Continuation of economic growth. Some economists argue that disharmony in economic relations between the United States and Japan is caused by excessively high economic growth in Japan and that decreasing the rate of growth would eliminate the disharmony. Other economists argue that, to arrest its adverse balance of payments, the United States should take a strong deflationary policy and reduce imports.

Neither of these arguments, however, presents the real solution to the problem. Decreasing Japan's economic growth rate arbitrarily and suppressing strong latent growing potential by reducing overseas markets would cause serious dissatisfaction among the Japanese people. Moreover, a lower growth rate in Japan would naturally tend to reduce the market for imports, thus making difficulties for those nations whose main export markets are Japan. For example, when Japan's growth rate decreased in recent years from 10 percent to 6 percent (1971), exports to Japan from the United States, Australia, Canada, and other countries also decreased, thereby compounding the balance of payments difficulties. Similarly, the protectionist movement in the United States became strong in 1970 when the U.S. growth rate declined and unemployment became acute.

Thus, if Japan and the United States are to maintain harmonious trade relations, the first condition must be that both countries continue to develop fully their latent growth potential, unhampered by restrictions imposed in the interests of achieving trade balances. Equalization of growth rates does not necessarily effect an equalization in balance of payments. For example, some calculate that the most desirable condition for balancing Japanese exports to the United

welfare and personal consumption to increase so that products are absorbed in the domestic market. This would probably result in a diversion of export products to the domestic market or an increase in imports or both. However, the argument that the Japanese economy depends too heavily on exporting does not appear to be substantiated in fact. In 1970 the ratio of exports to GNP was 9.9 percent and of imports to GNP 8.0 percent (see Table 4). In relation to other countries, Japan's percentage of exports is far from being excessive and is in fact rather low. Rather than strive to decrease exports, Japan should seek more imports.

5. *A more elastic exchange rate.* One of the most effective means at Japan's disposal to adjust its international balance of payments is the manipulation of the exchange rate. Between 1971 and 1973 in a series of adjustments the value of the yen was adjusted upward and the dollar downward. In a matter of months the large trade discrepencies between the two countries began to disappear, although Japan may continue to maintain some export excess because of the differences in the export structures of the two countries. This lesson has taught both countries the value of frequent currency adjustments to reverse trends toward serious trade imbalance.

When economic growth rate, inflation, industrial structure, and demand structure are all in a state of change in both countries, an equilibrium in balance of payments cannot be achieved under a fixed exchange rate. The future parity system must permit frequent changes of exchange rates so that worldwide adjustments can be made continuously in response to changing circumstances.

6. *Orderly marketing.* In those cases where the export of a certain commodity increases so sharply and so quickly as to threaten seriously the industry of the country to which it is

exported, voluntary control should be exercised in the exporting country, at least over the short run. However, this is an exceptional measure to be invoked under a situation of free trade and the conditions and procedures for its operation would have to be subjected to full investigation. It is probably true that shortrun control would make it possible for this type of imbalance to even out naturally in the long term.

7. *Export of capital.* Another effective means of offsetting a surplus in commodity trade is the encouragement of invisible trade and overseas investment. In other words, the ultimate goal of the two members of a bilateral trade relationship should be to balance the total account, not merely the commodity trade account. Dramatic and visible increases in Japanese direct investment in the U.S. economy have been an important factor in the recent reversal of the spiraling trade imbalance.

8. *Multilateral equilibrium.* Countries involved in a substantial bilateral trade relationship should not let an obsession with the bilateral balance of payments obscure the importance of the larger, multilateral equilibrium in balance of payments. For example, Japan inevitably suffers a balance of payments deficit with the Middle East and Australia because of its heavy importation of petroleum and mineral resources (see Table 5). With rapidly rising prices, this situation can only get worse. It follows that Japan's trade account with other countries, such as the United States, must run a surplus in order to cope with these deficits. Merely pursuing bilateral equilibrium serves to hinder the expansion of world trade.

9. *Foreign aid.* The Japanese government has been looking, in particular, to enlarged overseas aid programs to reduce the surplus in current accounts. Considering the expanding income gap between Japan and most of Southeast Asia, as

well as the population pressures on these countries, it is in Japan's interests to greatly increase future assistance in this area.

THE DEGREE OF CHANGE REQUIRED

We must now consider the degree to which these changes should be made in order to maintain harmonious U.S.-Japanese trade relations. Naturally, there are innumerable combinations of factors. One of the most recent Japanese forecasts projected the future relationship as follows: [1]

1. Both countries are likely to enjoy favorable economic growth. This assumes that the average growth rate for Japan between 1970 and 1980 will be 10 percent in real terms and 14 percent in nominal terms (the growth rate is based on yen; it would be 17 percent based on dollars), while the U.S. growth rate for the same period is presumed to average 4.5 percent in real terms and 7.1 percent in nominal terms.

2. To prevent the trade imbalance between the two countries from becoming extremely large, the annual increase rate of Japanese exports to the United States will have to be decreased, for example, from 18.4 percent to 16.1 percent between 1970 and 1980. At the same time, that of imports from the United States should be increased from 12.4 percent to 16.1 percent, thus balancing exports with imports (see Table 6).

3. For the same reason, Japan's dependence on imports should be increased, while decreasing dependence on exports. Japan's dependence on imports (that is, import/GNP) was 8 percent in 1970 and should be increased to 10 percent by 1980 (at the 1970 exchange rate).

4. In order to achieve increased dependence on imports and decreased dependence on exports it is necessary to adjust

the exchange rate. (It is assumed here that the yen is to be revalued from 360 yen to 280 yen per dollar.)

5. The relative weight of Japan's domestic agricultural production should be decreased as that of the service industry is increased.

6. The percentage of finished goods imported should be increased through trade liberalization and reduced customs duty.

7. The percentage of agricultural produce imported should be increased.

8. Japan's favorable balance in commodity trade, if it exists, should be offset by an adverse balance in invisible trade, overseas investment, foreign assistance, and so on.

9. In regard to U.S.-Japanese trade, Japan should increase its imports of food, raw materials, chemical products, machinery, and so on. As wages in Japan level off in the future, the market for U.S. industrial products in Japan should expand.

10. If it is possible to effect these changes, Japan's balance of payments will equalize as shown in Table 7. Although a trade imbalance will still exist between Japan and the United States, it will only be about 5 percent of total U.S. exports, which can be offset by invisible and multilateral trade (see Table 8).

CHANGES SINCE 1972

The trade imbalance between Japan and the United States began to reduce itself quickly in the beginning of 1973, and the year closed with a surplus in Japan's favor of a mere $200 million as compared with $3 billion in 1972. There appear to be two reasons for this phenomenon. One is the adjustments in exchange rates. In February 1973 the United States devalued the dollar against the SDR (special drawing right) by 10 percent and Japan floated the yen. This resulted in an exchange rate of 265 yen to the dollar, or a 16.23 percent appreciation of the yen over the basic rate of 308 yen to the dollar that had been agreed upon at the Smithsonian Institution meeting of December 1971. Although the yen began to weaken gradually thereafter, so that in early 1973 the exchange rate was 300 yen to the dollar, it is presumed that exchange rate adjustments contributed significantly to the correction in the lopsided balance of international payments.

The second reason was sharp upsurges in the price of farm products and raw and crude materials. Prices for wheat, corn, soybeans, lumber, and so on, rose substantially in 1973. Because the price elasticities of the demand for these commodities are small, Japan's payments for imports from the United States increased as much as 58 percent over the previous year.

As a result of these changes, the problem of trade imbalance, which had been a central point of controversy between the two countries since the early 1970's, declined in urgency. However, a number of new problems have arisen.

One of them is mounting anxiety in Japan as to whether the United States can assure Japan a stable supply of lumber, steel scrap, wheat, soybeans, feed grain, and so forth. In the summer of 1973 the United States imposed restrictions on the export of soybeans and their products. In Japan this gave rise to the argument that, if the United States is to restrict unilaterally the export of farm products in order to meet domestic demands, it is risky for Japan to continue to rely on the United States for the supply of these products. Opinions for raising the self-sufficiency ratio in Japan are gaining strength. If this trend should spread, it will serve to contract world trade.

A second problem is the impact that the oil crisis, which

had its advent in the summer of 1973, would have on U.S.-Japanese trade. The proportion of oil in Japan's total imports was 18 percent in 1973. It is expected to increase to nearly 30 percent in 1974, due to a vast rise in prices. Consequently, the question has arisen of whether this will increase Japan's unfavorable balance of trade with the Middle and Near East to the point where Japan may be forced to increase her favorable balance in trade with the United States by increasing exports to the United States or restricting imports from the United States. This might involve the risk that new tensions will develop between Japan and the United States.

Solutions to these problems will require, presumably, a reexamination of a desirable future structure of worldwide divisions of labor, not only from the standpoint of Japan and the United States, but also from a global point of view.

Table 1. U.S.-Japanese trade patterns ($ million)

	Japan's exports to the United States			Japan's imports from the United States		
	1960	1970	Magnification rate		1960	1970	Magnification rate
Portable electric calculators	—	77		Kaoliang	2	134	67
Television sets	1	265	265	Lumber	26	518	20
Automobiles	3	536	179	Corn	11	218	20
Bicycles	2	280	140	Electronic computers	7	138	20
Tape recorders	6	256	43	Coal	92	623	6.8
Iron–steel	75	899	12	Aircraft	41	245	6.0
Radios	71	397	5.6	Iron ore	13	49	3.8
Metal products	69	324	4.7	Soybeans	103	330	3.2
Apparel	116	274	2.4	Wheat	63	174	2.8
Ceramics	38	89	2.3	Pulp	24	64	2.7
Woolen fabrics	23	43	1.9	Scrap iron–steel	156	270	1.7
Footwear	49	81	1.7	Phosphate ore	21	36	1.7
Toys	54	78	1.4	Metal-processing machinery	41	69	1.7
Veneer	46	50	1.1	Petroleum products	77	110	1.4
				Cotton	221	80	0.4

Source: Ministry of Finance, "Monthly Return of Foreign Trade of Japan," December 1970.

Table 2. U.S.-Japanese Bilateral Trade

Year	Japan's trade with the United States ($ million)			Percentage of Japan's export to U.S. among her total export	Percentage of Japan's import from U.S. among her total import	Percentage of U.S. export to Japan among her total export	Percentage of U.S. import from Japan among her total import
	Export (FOB)	Import (CIF)	Balance				
1950	183	434	−251	22.3	44.6	4.3	2.0
1960	1102	1554	−452	27.2	34.6	7.9	7.3
61	1067	2096	−1.029	25.2	36.1	10.4	7.2
62	1400	1809	−409	28.5	32.1	8.6	8.5
63	1507	2077	−570	27.6	36.2	9.2	8.9
64	1842	2336	−494	27.6	29.4	9.0	9.8
65	2479	2366	113	29.3	30.0	8.8	11.6
66	2969	2658	311	30.4	27.9	9.0	11.6
67	3012	3212	−200	28.8	27.5	10.4	11.2
68	4086	3527	559	31.5	27.2	10.4	12.3
69	4958	4090	868	31.0	27.2	11.0	13.8
70	5940	5560	380	30.7	29.4	13.0	14.9
71	7495	4978	2517	31.2	25.3	11.4	16.4
72	8856	5848	3008	30.9	24.9	10.0	16.3
73	9460	9257	203	25.6	24.2	—	—

Source: Ministry of Finance, "Summary Report of Japanese Trade," published by Japan Tariff Association, 1972.

Table 3. Difficulties in future U.S.-Japanese trade ($ billion) (simple extrapolation of trade in 1960-70)

		1960	1970	1980	rate of growth 1960-70
JAPAN	GNP	44.9	196.2	798.3	15.9
	Export to U.S. (FOB)	1.1	6.0	32.7	18.4
	Import from U.S. (FOB)	1.4	4.6	15.1	12.4
U.S.	GNP	511.4	976.5	1865.1	6.7
	Export to Japan	1.4	4.6	15.1	12.4
	Import from Japan	1.1	6.0	32.7	18.4
JAPAN	Total export	4.1	19.3	90.9	16.9
	Total import	3.9	15.7	63.3	15.0
U.S.	Total export	20.4	42.6	89.0	7.6
	Total import	14.8	38.9	102.3	10.1
JAPAN	Export ratio to U.S. %	27.4	31.2	36.0	—
	Import ratio from U.S. %	37.1	29.4	23.9	—
U.S.	Export ratio to Japan %	6.9	10.8	17.0	—
	Import ratio from Japan %	7.4	15.4	32.0	—
Balance of U.S.-Japan trade		−0.3	1.4	17.6	—
Ratio of surplus to Japan's GNP %		−0.7	0.7	2.2	—
JAPAN	Export to U.S./GNP	2.5	3.1	4.1	—
	Import from U.S./GNP	3.1	2.3	1.9	—
	Total export/GNP	9.1	9.8	11.4	—
	Total import/GNP	8.7	8.0	7.9	—
U.S.	Export to Japan/GNP	0.3	0.5	0.8	—
	Import from Japan/GNP	0.2	0.6	1.8	—
	Total export/GNP	4.0	4.4	4.8	—
	Total import/GNP	2.9	4.0	5.5	—

Sources: Economic Planning Agency, "Annual Report on National Income Statistics, 1972"; Bank of Japan, "Balance of Payments Monthly"; U.S. Department of Commerce, "Survey of Current Business"; and Japan Economic Research Center, "A Long-Term Outlook of Japanese and U.S. Economies," March 1973, pp. 8-10.

Table 4. World economy and Japan's exports and imports

	1960	1970	1980
World GNP ($ billion)	1,405	3,049	7,643
		(8.2)[a]	(9.6)
Japan's GNP ($ billion)	43	196	957
		(16.5)	(17.2)
World trade ($ billion)	128	311	850
		(9.3)	(10.6)
Japan's exports ($ billion)[b]	4.1	19.3	92.2
		(16.9)	(16.9)
Japan's imports ($ billion)	3.9	15.7	75.5
		(15.0)	(17.0)
Ratio of Japan's dependency on exports	9.4	9.9	9.6
Ratio of Japan's dependency on imports	9.0	8.0	7.9
Elasticity of Japan's exports to world trade		1.82	1.59
Elasticity of Japan's imports to income		0.91	0.98
Japan's export share in world trade (percent)	3.2	6.2	10.8

Source: Japan Economic Research Center, "Japan's Economy in 1980 in the Global Context," March 1972, p. 4.

[a]Figures in parentheses are average rates of increase in the preceding 10 years.

[b]Both exports and imports are in FOB values.

Table 5. Japanese imports, composition by commodity and origin (percent)[a]

Trade area	Food and beverages SITC (0.1)	Raw materials (2.4)	Mineral fuels (3)	Chemicals (5)	Machinery & equipment (7)	Other manufactures (6.8)	Total
Advanced area, total	57.3 (60.5)	50.7 (52.3)	15.5 (19.5)	91.6 (90.9)	95.2 (97.0)	54.6 (54.5)	56.4 (54.0)
U.S.	25.9 (33.9)	23.3 (23.2)	6.7 (12.6)	43.2 (44.2)	60.1 (61.4)	21.2 (22.0)	27.8 (27.7)
Canada	4.9 (5.2)	7.1 (8.6)	0.3 (0.5)	3.7 (2.5)	5.7 (0.8)	1.3 (4.8)	3.6 (4.6)
(European Community)	5.9 (3.4)	0.6 (0.7)	0.0 (0.0)	26.9 (25.4)	20.1 (20.5)	11.2 (10.2)	9.0 (5.9)
EFTA (European Tree Trade Area)	4.8 (1.9)	1.4 (0.7)	0.0 (0.0)	16.0 (14.5)	9.0 (14.0)	10.5 (10.2)	6.2 (4.4)
Western Europe, total	11.2 (5.9)	2.1 (1.6)	0.0 (0.1)	43.8 (40.6)	29.4 (34.8)	22.2 (21.5)	15.5 (10.7)
ANS (Australia, New Zealand, South Africa)	15.3 (15.1)	18.2 (18.9)	8.5 (6.5)	0.9 (3.6)	0.0 (0.1)	9.9 (6.2)	9.5 (11.0)

Developing area, total	24.6 (35.6)	32.9 (39.5)	77.8 (77.2)	4.9 (5.8)	2.6 (2.0)	35.4 (40.3)	33.9 (40.6)
Southeast Asia	7.3 (20.3)	22.8 (23.7)	14.0 (9.3)	4.0 (4.2)	2.1 (1.6)	18.3 (16.4)	13.6 (15.4)
West Asia	0.3 (0.3)	0.5 (0.4)	61.4 (66.1)	0.3 (0.3)	0.0 (0.0)	1.6 (1.5)	12.1 (13.8)
Latin America	13.8 (12.4)	6.7 (10.2)	0.7 (0.9)	0.3 (1.0)	0.2 (0.0)	4.4 (6.0)	4.0 (6.3)
Africa	2.9	2.0 (3.9)	1.4 (0.2)	0.3 (0.1)	0.3 (0.4)	10.9 (16.8)	4.0 (4.2)
Others	0.3 (0.3)	0.9 (1.4)	0.3 (0.6)	0.0 (0.1)	0.0 (0.0)	0.2 (0.5)	0.2 (0.7)
Planned economy bloc	18.1 (3.8)	16.6 (8.2)	6.7 (3.3)	3.4 (2.9)	2.2 (0.9)	10.1 (5.3)	9.7 (5.4)
Total	100.0 (100.0)	100.0 (100.0)	100.0 (100.0)	100.0 (100.0)	100.0 (100.0)	100.0 (100.0)	100.0 (100.0)

Source: Japan Economic Research Center, "Japan's Economy in 1980 in the Global Context," March 1972, p. 36.

[a]Upper figures are projected values for 1980 and lower ones actual values for 1969.

Sources: Calculated from UN-MBS and Matrix by commodity.

Table 6. Japan-U.S. trade by commodity ($ million)[a]

SITC	Japan's Exports to United States				
	1965	1969	1980	1965-69	1969-80
0-9 Total	2,510	5,020	26,751	18.9	16.4
	(100.0)	(100.0)	(100.0)		
0.1 Foodstuffs	98	125	251	6.3	6.5
	(3.9)	(2.5)	(0.9)		
2.4 Raw materials	59	35	47	−12.2	2.7
	(2.4)	(0.7)	(0.2)		
3 Mineral fuels	3	5	13	13.6	9.1
	(0.1)	(0.1)	(0.0)		
5 Chemicals	46	130	1,374	29.7	23.8
	(1.8)	(2.6)	(5.1)		
7 Machinery	575	1,830	16,879	33.6	22.4
	(22.9)	(36.5)	(63.1)		
6.8 Other manufactures	1,710	2,850	8,187	13.6	10.1
	(68.1)	(56.8)	(30.6)		

SITC	Japan's Imports from United States				
	1965	1969	1980	1965-69	1969-80
0-9 Total	2,070	3,460	20,956	13.7	17.8
	(100.0)	(100.0)	(100.0)		
0.1 Foodstuffs	510	600	1,770	4.2	10.3
	(24.6)	(17.3)	(8.4)		
2.4 Raw materials	670	960	3,604	9.4	12.8
	(32.4)	(27.7)	(17.2)		
3 Mineral fuels	140	320	955	23.0	10.4
	(6.8)	(9.2)	(4.6)		
5 Chemicals	150	305	1,891	19.4	18.1
	(7.2)	(8.8)	(9.0)		
7 Machinery	415	810	8,330	18.2	23.6
	(20.0)	(23.4)	(39.7)		
6.8 Other manufactures	155	420	4,406	28.1	24.1
	(7.5)	(12.1)	(21.0)		

Source: Japan Economic Research Center, "Japan's Economy in 1980 in the Global Context," March 1972, p. 38.

[a]Figures in parentheses are percent of total. Figures in the right two columns are rates of growth.
Source: UN-MBS.

Table 7. Japan's balance of international payments ($ million, 1980 projected)

	1961	1965	1970	1980
Trade balance	−558	1,901	3,963	16,674
Exports (fob)	4,149	8,332	18,969	92,184
Imports (fob)	4,707	6,431	15,006	75,510
Services	−383	−884	−1,785	−5,965
Credits	1,016	1,563	4,009	22,766
Debits	1,399	2,447	5,794	28,731
Transfers	−41	−85	−208	−2,738
(Government grant)	(−105)	(−96)	(−179)	(−2,326)
Current balance	982	932	1,970	7,971
Long-term capital	−11	−415	−1,591	−7,971
Assets	−312	−446	−2,031	−14,704
Liabilities	301	31	440	6,733
(Direct foreign investment)	(−94)	(−77)	(−355)	(−4,500)
Basic balance	−993	517	379	0
Overall balance	−952	405	1,374	0
Gold & foreign exchange reserve	1,666	2,152	4,839	

Source: Japan Economic Research Center, "Japan's Economy in 1980 in the Global Context," March 1972, p. 12.

Table 8. Japan's balance of international trade with the United States ($ million, 1980 projected)

	1960	1970	1980	Increase rate % 1960-70	1970-80
Trade balance	440	1,410	5,795	–	–
Japan's exports to U.S. (fob)	2,510	6,020	26,751	18.4	16.1
Japan's imports from U.S. (fob)	2,070	4,610	20,956	12.4	16.1

Source: Table 7.

5

HENRY ROSOVSKY

Japan and the United States:
Notes from the Devil's Advocate

Relations between Japan and the Western world are.not in a
healthy state, and the events of the early 1970's have not laid
the foundation for an early recovery. There can be little
doubt, for example, that the President's economic moves of
1971—the "Nixon shocks"—in spite of their multilateral
framework, were aimed primarily at the Japanese. The domestic attitude in the United States to Japan's economic
prowess of the last decade has unmistakably acquired strong
reactionary overtones. A recent advertising campaign sponsored by the International Ladies' Garment Workers Union
featured those two sacred symbols of our national heritage,
the American flag and the baseball glove, bearing made-in-
Japan labels. We might also remember the reaction to Secretary George Schultz's speech at the International Monetary
Fund meetings in Washington in 1972: his ideas on future
international monetary arrangements were warmly received
by everyone present (including the French) except the Japanese. Finally, let us keep in mind the general European
attitude toward Japan, most aptly summed up by the question: how can we keep the Japanese out of our hair?

What has led to this deterioration? Obviously it could not

have been the effects of Japanese foreign policy, since until very recently Japan has had nothing of the kind. Nor can we blame aggressive nationalistic or military ambitions on the part of Japan, since these have been nonexistent. The deterioration must be related to two fundamental changes that have taken place in the last twenty years: Japan's economic success and changing domestic circumstances in the United States, with the fears and uncertainties these have generated.

Japan has the second largest GNP in the free world with a per capita GNP of over $2,000 and will be a major factor in the world economy, on par with the EEC, the Soviet Union, and way ahead of China, for the rest of our lives. Consequently, it is not very fruitful to think of Japan primarily as an irritant, a scapegoat for our own national failures, or a whipping boy for special interest groups. Instead, we should attempt to understand what happened in Japan in the recent past, what is likely to happen in the near future, and, most of all, what the implications of Japan's future are for the United States and for the rest of the world. I would like to make a few observations concerning each of these points.

JAPANESE ECONOMIC GROWTH

Japan's economic performance from the early 1950's to 1970 exceeded that of any other comparable economy during this period. We have become accustomed to referring to this phenomenon as Japan's "economic miracle:" a real average rate of growth of GNP of 10 percent per year, productivity increases in key industries reaching 20 percent per year, and waves of attractive Japanese products sweeping the markets of the world. An annual expansion of 6 percent would be termed a "severe recession" for Japan. Obviously, this success was not the result of a single magic formula but of a number of conditions and elements that formed a complex, dynamic relationship. There are no economic miracles; what has happened in the past can be explained rationally.

In the case of Japan, economic success has been mainly the story of massive inflows of foreign technology and its ingenious adaptations to Japanese industry. With other conditions for industrial growth extremely favorable during the period from 1950 to 1970, the selective and concentrated application of foreign technology, which was almost always superior to that available in Japan, permitted industrial modernization and innovation at an unprecedented rate. In short, Japan became a businessman's paradise.

The components of that paradise are quite readily indentifiable:

1. The technological gap between Japan and the more advanced countries presented Japanese entrepreneurs with great and obvious opportunities. Foreigners were willing and anxious to sell their know-how under favorable royalty and license arrangements. Japanese business and government both were intent on pursuing a course that would keep foreign enterprise out of the Japanese market and that would also avoid the costly and risky process of research and development. The direct purchase of foreign processes and their systematic adaptation to Japanese industrial development was the logical and most compelling choice. My intention is not to stress the imitative nature of Japan's economic achievements. On the contrary, I have always been most impressed with the creative aspects of borrowing technology, which were raised to a fine art in Japan. Through a process that may be called "improvement engineering" Japanese industrialists frequently studied and improved the components of this imported technology and made it work even more effectively under the Japanese system. In some cases, rela-

tively minor Japanese improvements increased the performance of foreign processes to 130 percent of rated capacity.

2. The labor situation was also extremely favorable for the Japanese businessman. Workers of high quality were available at reasonable wages. The input of foreign technology which resulted in better equipment and increased output did not, at the same time, produce pressures for comparable wage increases. Until the late 1960's, labor strikes were inconsequential and Japanese unions appeared to be more interested in "American imperialism" or relations with mainland China than working conditions on the shop floor. Thus cost pressures were kept at a minimum while productivity rose at an average annual rate of 9 percent. No doubt, American businessmen would have relished such labor conditions: during the same period, wage increases in the United States and Europe often exceeded increases in productivity.

3. The government contributed to the businessman's paradise by doing whatever seemed necessary to maximize the rate of growth of GNP. Indeed, this seems to have been the major goal of Japan's entire national effort. Taxes were moderate, the Ministry of International Trade and Industry backed a variety of imaginative industrial policies, and defense expenditures were kept below 1 percent of GNP. In contrast with the United States, Japanese government and business cooperated in the pursuit of common goals. Selected growth industries were primed through the control of foreign exchange allocations and foreign technology inflow. Perhaps one should also add a "negative" government contribution: welfare continued to be a private matter in Japan. The individual was responsible for his children's education, for his own retirement, and for unforeseen emergencies. Undoubtedly, this situation encouraged private savings, which in the 1960's represented about 20 percent of disposable income, compared with 7 percent in the United States. The high rate

of savings in Japan has been crucial to sustaining the level of plant and equipment investment necessary for the growth of output.

4. Finally, a most crucial element of the paradise has been the external situation: an undervalued currency, exports growing 2.5 times as rapidly as world trade, and technology and resource imports available under favorable conditions. The climate for trade expansion was particularly encouraging during this period, with Japan's largest customer, the United States, the leading advocate of free trade. Foreign customers found Japanese goods to be most attractive in terms of price and quality. Furthermore, Japanese industry concentrated on those export commodities for which technological progress would be most likely to reduce cost, including transportation equipment, machinery, iron and steel. Undoubtedly, the absorption of foreign technology has promoted the rapid decline in capital-output ratios that most of these industries have experienced over the last few years. The Japanese government further stimulated the growth of competitive export industries through preferential credit rationing, tax exemptions, protection from overseas competition and preference in the import of foreign technology.

It would be a mistake to assume, however, that Japan could have been a businessman's paradise without the businessman himself having superior qualities. Entrepreneurial talent had flowered in Japan during the past twenty years. By the time Japan went to war in 1941 one may speculate about the industrial order having become the victim of social rigidities that imposed considerations of age, class, and family or banking connections on new enterprise. World War II destroyed the rigidities of this order and gave rise to a situation in which imagination and innovation are at a premium, regardless of background. Thus a strong "new" entrepreneurial class had developed in Japan and, by the yardstick of performance, has done brilliant service to the cause of Japanese economic growth.

THE PROSPECT FOR THE 1970'S

Today forecasters still seem to be suffering from the same errors of prediction that 30 years ago led to projections of a bleak economic future for Japan. In the aftermath of the defeat and destruction of World War II, Japan's large population and sparse natural resources were supposed to be insurmountable obstacles to economic growth and independence. The United States prepared itself to assume a portion of Japan's economic burden for the indefinite future. On the basis of a straight projection of trends current at that time, this made sense to economists. However, they had overlooked the possibility of rapid absorption of technology in Japan, which, as we have seen, was really a most critical variable.

The same straight projections were being made until late 1973 to predict the world's largest GNP for Japan by the year 2000. Japan is expected to surpass the United States in both industrial productivity and standard of living. Such predictions, however, as those of the late 1940's, are based on the critical assumption that the current economic trends will continue full speed ahead for the next 30 years. But a review of the past and an understanding of the present should convince most observers that the ingredients of Japan's paradise no longer look the same today. Chances are that conditions will have altered even more by the end of the 1970's.

Let us consider in turn each of the elements that contributed to the paradisiac conditions of the 1950's and 1960's:

1. The technology gap is nearly closed and will almost certainly disappear entirely by the end of the 1970's. This

implies that the Japanese are beginning to face the same problems as other countries on the frontier of technological advance. Japanese business is already increasing its research and development expenditures and pursuing the development of its own advanced technology. Thus one can no longer judge future Japanese growth on the basis of the rates that applied while Japan was merely catching up to those in the lead. While Japan has so far been able to realize rapid gains by benefiting from the mistakes and the research and development expenditures of others, now that the gap is closing, further technological and industrial growth will have to depend more and more on the resources of Japanese industry. There will be mistakes, there will be wrong guesses, and above all, there will be increased costs. Success will not come as easily as it has in the past. This is not to suggest that the Japanese are less talented than others at pushing ahead the frontiers of knowledge; my assumption is that they are on a par with everyone else.

2. The changing labor situation in Japan is very well known. Japan has nearly reached zero population growth and the age structure of the population is rapidly shifting in favor of older people. The government has estimated that the working age population will rise by only 1 percent a year during the 1970's. At the same time, an expanding modern industry will need more workers. This is contributing in several ways to basic inflationary trends in Japan. There are no indications that the trends toward declining labor supply, rising wages, and thus higher costs, will reverse during the 1970's. The possible effects of this situation on organized labor bear warning. Whereas management has in the past exercised very little resistance to large wage increases, because they were more than matched by productivity, in the future, as productivity slackens, there is likely to be much resistance to wage increases. If, at that same time, living costs

continue to rise, and the labor supply is short, it seems safe
to assume that organized labor will become more militant.
The effect of a wave of major strikes on large employers
could, at some point, significantly disadvantage Japan's export capabilities.

3. There are also likely to be changes in the economic
policy of the Japanese government, where the growth-at-any-
cost philosophy may soon be a thing of the past. Lack of
social capital, pollution, demand for greater public welfare
measures are by now a familiar refrain in the public media in
Japan. Such issues are beginning to take on political overtones that could be ominous for the LDP, and it appears that
the government will have to respond soon and in significant
measure. Prime Minister Kakuei Tanaka, until very recently,
still seemed intent on maintaining very high growth rates and
improving social overhead capital at the same time, a difficult
task that would appear to risk greater inflation.

The problems to be overcome in this area are numerous.
Modern economic growth has brought Japan the world's
largest per area GNP, which means that no other country has
concentrated so much economic activity in so little space.
Pollution of all kinds is rampant. The government's policy of
emphasizing maximum rate of growth of aggregate output,
private capital formation, and a balanced budget has led to a
cumulative lag in public investment. Recent price increases,
especially the cost of labor and the inflation of land prices,
tend to aggravate the problem. Low taxes make it difficult to
make new funds available. There is also a deficiency in social
security in Japan, which, coupled with the declining birth
rate and consequent shift toward a higher proportion of old
people, suggests that a crisis in providing for the aged may
arise unless measures are taken immediately.

In the past, when efforts have been made to increase social
investment in Japan, they have been met with powerful

resistance from private enterprise, using its influence in the government to forestall the economic impact of improving the quality of life. In effect, increases in interest rates and corporate taxes have been avoided at substantial cost to social improvement. Those who have suffered the consequences have only recently begun to develop the machinery to bring their own pressures to bear on the government.

No one can today foresee the outcome of the present transition with great clarity. However, among its most probable consequences will be a higher government tax-take, a higher aggregate capital-output ratio, perhaps lower savings rates, and somewhat reduced output growth as investments shift to areas less directly contributing to growth by conventional measurements. It would be reasonable to expect more emphasis on the quality of life and a more internal orientation, all developing quite gradually.

4. Finally, the external situation has changed in a most dramatic manner and one cannot rule out the possibility that this will have significant effects on Japan's foreign trade. Protectionist sentiments are voiced more frequently in the United States and Western Europe. Asians are also voicing fears of political and economic "domination" by Japan. Meanwhile, Japan's appetite for raw materials is becoming gargantuan, and trends toward cost rises that are now apparent are bound to be reflected in export prices, which will not be to their competitive advantage in world markets. Figures published by the Japan Economic Research Center estimate that Japanese exports will represent 10 percent of total world exports by 1975, with 18 percent of the U.S. market and 35 percent of the Asian market. I question that this rate of expansion can be sustained during the latter half of the 1970's.

It is most important to understand that all these prospects for the 1970's are largely independent of the so-called energy crisis and the political events associated with the recent Middle Eastern war. One has to be careful not to confuse short-term crises with long-term trends, and much that has been written in and about Japan after October 1973 does just that. Some recent reports give the impression that Japan has suffered a national nervous breakdown; that the Japanese economy has gone into a tailspin from which it cannot possibly recover; that a shortage of oil will bring factories to a standstill; that current balance of payments difficulties cannot be overcome, and so on.

All this is pretty silly—just as silly as the notion that Japan would be able to sustain a 10 percent rate of growth forever. Although it is not possible to analyze the events after October 1973 in detail—far too little time has elapsed and the uncertainties remain very great—a few personal evaluations may be helpful. The fundamental problem appears to be the steep increase in the price of oil (*not* a physical shortage) and Japan's nearly total dependence on imports of this vital product. It is a serious matter, because Japan needs such large quantities of oil, and a quadrupling of the price has to lead to a great variety of cost changes, affected internal prices, and international comparative advantage. Furthermore, the balance of payments implications are also sizable; some highly preliminary estimates suggest that Japan may have to pay $10 billion *more* for oil in 1974.

Two conclusions can be made about the present situation. First, there really is no basis for any solid prediction concerning the next six months to one year. Nations that are today considered "friendly" by the Arabs, may—all of a sudden—be reinscribed on the "unfriendly" list. The oil price could come down if the cartel weakens. Perhaps the leading consumer nations can form a strong organization of their own. Another war in the Middle East is also possible. The list of eventualities is nearly endless, and therefore further speculation does not seem productive.

The second conclusion is that the recent events have reinforced many of the previously described trends—especially those related to Japan's external economic situation. Following two upward revaluations of the yen, Japan's accumulated surpluses had started to decline well before 1973. Similarly, the government has understood for a long time that an adequate supply of fuels and raw materials would create both economic and political difficulties. Government and business have also known for some years that certain industries were becoming less economical and therefore had to be shifted to places where labor was cheaper and pollution control less rigorous. But none of this spells disaster. On the contrary, the Japanese have always shown great adaptability to changing circumstances. They are, in many senses, far less ideological than Americans, and there is absolutely no reason to doubt their ability to bend with the wind.

Although the purpose of the preceding discussion has been to play the devil's advocate, as I have stated elsewhere, I am firmly convinced of the validity of the two major themes: "(1) that there are certain factors inherent in a higher level of economic maturity that will make it increasingly more difficult to maintain a real annual growth rate of 10 percent, and (2) that a government-financed improvement in the quality of life will have the same result."[1]

To put the matter in longer term perspective, we can say that between 1900 and 1970 Japan moved from backwardness to semi-development and this brought about *trend acceleration.* Between 1970 and the year 2000 Japan will move from semi-development to a mature economy and this implies gradual *trend deceleration.*[2] For the end of the 1970's I think a good guess would be a real growth rate of

GNP of about 7 percent a year, because the development opportunities are still very great—especially in the rationalization of the service sector and in improving standards of private consumption—although a great deal will depend on the outside world.

THE IMPLICATIONS OF TRANSITION

This view of the matter suggests a number of broad and difficult problems for ourselves, for the Japanese, and for third parties. Since the 1950's, Japan's economic growth has presented the world with what I believe to be a historically unique problem: a large and wealthy country, virtually without material resources, growing much more rapidly than the rest of the world. Furthermore, the industrial structure of that country and its "custom" mean that its economic development translates into a gigantic stream of attractively priced exports of manufactured products. Can the world—will the world—swallow these goods? Are we perhaps moving toward a situation in which Japan will champion free trade, while we and the Europeans will become the champions of restriction?

These days one sometimes hears it said by European and American businessmen and government officials that "special rules" are needed for dealing with Japan. After all, it is claimed, the Japanese are not like us. They have "Japan, Incorporated:" they cannot be trusted; they dump their products; they work too hard, and so on. Therefore, we require three sets of rules: one for our friends, one for the Communist countries, and one for Japan. In other words, practices that would not be permitted vis-à-vis the advanced countries of Europe—for example, quotas—would be quite all right when it come to Japanese products. What would be the consequences of such a state of affairs?

The question just posed can be broadened. Will the world

accept Japan as a world power? Or, will the Japanese once again be rejected? (For this is certainly how most Japanese interpret relations with the West during the past century.) I am not attempting to draw a contrast between "good" Japanese and "bad" Americans and Europeans. It could just as easily be asked: will the Japanese act as a mature world power, and have they understood that a large surplus is as bad as a chronic deficit? I am convinced that until very recently Japan did not today understand that it was in grave danger of rapidly becoming an "odd man out" in international economic relations.

The dangers are clear, especially during the transitional period of the 1970's. By the end of the 70's we may reasonably expect a Japanese economy somewhat reoriented domestically, much closer to a European-type welfare state, and growing at more reasonable levels. But for the next five or eight years, we will certainly continue to face a large and wealthy country importing primarily raw materials and exporting primarily manufactures. Not making room for Japan may have its attractions, particularly for certain entrepreneurs and workers in a variety of competing industries. Consumers who buy attractive Japanese products obviously will be somewhat less delighted if we fail to make room. However, leaving aside the benefits of international competition that we would be giving up and the consequences of restrictionism on our own society, we should understand that the political price of excluding Japan is likely to be very high. I can see greater instability in Asia, a new type of undesirable regionalism, and adverse political consequences within Japan.

The task of integrating Japan is delicate and difficult. What we in the United States most need right now is a policy that takes into account Japan's economic transition of the 1970's. And what the Japanese need is a willingness to pay their fair share of the costs during this transitional period. Unfortunately, I am not able to suggest the precise outlines of such a policy at this time. Clearly, the Japanese will have to restructure their economy toward open markets, and the imports of manufactures and agricultural products. The United States should continue to retain its own open economy, but we must pay far more attention to transferring workers and capital out of uncompetitive industries. The cost of this process should not be simply imposed on the owners of these businesses or on the workers, but perhaps should be *shared* by our government and the Japanese government. Any agreement of this type would be a historical breakthrough and also a very welcome innovation.

In some ways, the situation is more hopeful now in 1974 than it was in 1971. For their part, the Japanese have continued energetically to open their economy, and a certain amount of internal restructuring in the right direction is occurring. Their surpluses are not nearly as large as they were a few years ago and still seem to be declining. And the major economic powers have become somewhat more acclimatized to floating exchange rates: trade flows have not been interrupted, and no one can point to large-scale disasters. Even the so-called energy crisis may have a positive effect on U.S.-Japanese relations. After all, it is—in many ways—a common problem that may make it easier to see questions in a more global context.

In the United States, it seems to me that we have also become rather more sensitive to Japan in the past year or so. The extreme advocates of protectionism have not prevailed in Congress. The administration appears to be consulting more actively with Tokyo, and the appointment of Secretary of State Kissinger may place the State Department in somewhat greater prominence, and that is another positive thing for U.S.-Japanese relations. We seem to be anxious to mend our fences.

Nevertheless, one should not be overly impressed with short-run improvements: short-run deteriorations are just as likely. We do need, jointly, to develop a policy for the 1970's that recognizes the structural problems involved in absorbing a rapidly expanding Japan into the economic world order. That requires long-range planning concerning U.S.-Japanese economic relations. If this process is really taking place at anything resembling adequate levels of effort, it must be one of the best kept secrets in Washington and Tokyo.

6

DWIGHT H. PERKINS

Asian Economic Growth:

The Influence of the

United States and Japan

For a decade and more large parts of East and Southeast Asia have been undergoing rapid economic development. Where in late nineteenth and early twentieth century Europe rates of growth of 4 or 5 percent per year were considered to be "high," today in Asia annual increases of 9 and 10 percent are almost commonplace. Japan has, of course, led the way. In the early 1950's Japan was still really a less developed nation with a per capita income of around U.S. $300. Twenty years later Japan has become one of three economic giants with a per capita income higher than that of most of the nations of Western Europe.

The Japanese case is well known. The implications of what is happening in the rest of East and Southeast Asia are not so readily apparent, but it is becoming increasingly clear that many of these nations, too, are moving from a stage of underdevelopment into the status of highly industrialized states. The city-states of Singapore and Hong Kong with per capita incomes well above U.S. $1000 have already achieved this status. If past growth trends continue, Taiwan, South

Korea and others may not be far behind. The simple effects of compound interest illustrate what is happening. At a 2 percent annual rate of increase, income doubles in about four decades. At 7 percent doubling occurs in one decade and in three decades income increases eightfold. Thus what it took the Europeans and Americans one to two centuries to accomplish, is now occurring in parts of Asia in a fraction of that time. It is occurring, that is, if present trends continue and if other nations in the region also begin to experience accelerated growth.

There is little doubt that these developments in Asia directly affect the interests of both the United States and Japan, but more the latter than the former. Political stability in the region, for example, is more important to a nation separated from the rest of Asia by the Straits of Tsushima than it is to one separated by the Pacific Ocean.

The difference in the relative stakes of the two countries is even more apparent in the economic sphere. In the area of trade, for example, 25 percent of Japan's exports are sold to the nations of eastern and southern Asia, and some 16 percent of her imports are obtained from the region. The comparable U.S. figures are 9 and 8.5 percent respectively (in 1970), and even this wide disparity does not bring out fully the two countries' differing stakes. Total trade is roughly twice as high a percentage of Japan's GNP as it is of America's. In the making of foreign policy, whether rationally or otherwise, Americans generally relegate economic considerations to a secondary position. In contrast, Japanese foreign policy has at times seemed to be governed by little else. The greater importance of trade together with Japan's comparatively recent rise from poverty probably goes a long way toward explaining this difference in behavior.

If one turns from the question of interests to the means by which Japan and the United States have attempted to accomplish their aims in Asia, economics plays an even larger role. The accelerating Japanese aid program is the most conspicuous example of the place of economics in the foreign policy strategies of the two countries in Asia, but there is much more. America's gradual military pullback from Asia is not being matched at the economic level in either the governmental or private sphere. In spite of the overall cutback in American aid appropriations, U.S. aid to Indonesia was greatly expanded following the 1965 coup and has been maintained at a high level to date. More important than aid from either Japan or the United States has been the two nations' rapidly expanding trade with the region. Japanese and American exports to eastern and southern Asia which had reached a level of $3,510 million in 1960 had expanded to $8,925 million by 1970. Imports from the region had risen from $1,950 million to $6,415 million. In addition to trade, private investors have been becoming increasingly involved in the area.

The remainder of this essay is an attempt to come to grips with the issue of whether the increasing American and Japanese economic involvement in Asia is in the two countries' broader political as well as economic interests. The central question asked, in brief, is whether the economic policies being pursued at present are in the 1970's likely to contribute to relatively stable economic, political, and social progress in the region.

But, in order to study the effects of Japanese-American aid and trade, it is first necessary to have some understanding of economic and social developments in the region over the past decade. Because much of what has been happening is not well known, the next section is devoted to an analysis of some relevant aspects of these developments. With these as background, we then return to the question of the likely future effects of Japanese and American economic involvement.

ECONOMIC TRENDS IN ASIA

Even a casual acquaintance with the recent economic experience of the various Asian states is enough to make it clear that no single pattern explains the successes of some or the failures of others. Some generalizations, however, are possible.

Generalizations are most easily arrived at for those parts of Asia that did not grow rapidly or at all. Indochina requires little discussion. Even if growth has occurred in South Vietnam among the ravages of war, it has been growth artificially stimulated by massive war-related expenditures and tells little or nothing about the country's future prospects once the fighting has stopped.

Indonesia in the early 1960's spent large sums on military adventures and other unproductive areas (for example, the stadiums for the Asian games). The resulting hyperinflation, together with mismanagement of the economy in general, effectively foreclosed the possibility of growth. Since the 1965 coup the government has had its hands full overcoming the inflation and the most flagrant areas of mismanagement and neglect. Whether it will succeed in these endeavors and whether success will be followed by sustained increases in per capita income remains to be seen.

The Burmese push toward socialism, which began in the 1950's, has itself been an obstacle to growth in part because of the difficulties inherent in any attempt to introduce state ownership and control of commerce and industry in a country with a bureaucracy unprepared for the task. Socialism in Burma, however, was also a device for expropriating "alien," that is, Chinese and Indian, businesses. Since entrepreneurial experience and skills were a near monopoly of these communities, the economic effects of their exclusion from so many areas of business activity were predictable and pronounced.

What the examples of Indonesia and Burma demonstrate is that a political climate hostile to the private sector can quickly bring growth in that sector to a halt (or prevent it from starting up). If the government, in addition, is incapable of or unwilling to provide an effective substitute, economic development simply does not take place—a conclusion that should surprise almost no one.

If a hostile political climate is inimical to growth, it has been far from obvious in the past that a climate favorable to private sector enterprise would lead to rapid economic development in these countries. But the events of this last decade require some revision in the widely held belief that economic and social barriers made economic prospects bleak even if the political climate were favorable. One of the principal characteristics that the fast developers of East and Southeast Asia have had in common has been a fair degree of political stability and a government favorably disposed toward the private sector. Beyond this, however, most of these governments have had little in common. At one end of the spectrum is the Singapore government of Lee Kuan-yew or the government of Malaysia freely elected in more or less open competition with other parties. At the other end is the Kuomintang government on Taiwan dependent on the traditional sources of power of the authoritarian state or perhaps the undisguised colonial government of Hong Kong. In between are such combinations of elections and military coups as those that brought the present South Korean government to power and have kept it there.

With such widely differing kinds of political systems, it is not surprising to discover that there were also differences in the economic policies that led to growth. As a result, it is no easy matter to pinpoint what it was in the efforts of these nations that led to rapid development, but the effort to discern a pattern is necessary if we are to talk about the effects of Japanese and American policies to aid the process.

One can begin by noting that most of the countries that have achieved economic success have had a large stock of educated personnel for some time, whereas Indonesia, by way of contrast, had only a handful of trained Indonesians at the time of independence. The differences between Dutch, British, Japanese, and American colonial educational efforts had something to do with this disparity, but probably a more important factor was the high value placed on education by the Chinese and Korean tradition (and the disproportionate share of educated in the exodus to Hong Kong and Taiwan after 1949). Much of the education that did take place in the region prior to say 1950 was in privately financed, not government schools. When the decision was finally made to expand the public system, the personnel to staff that expansion were available in more or less adequate numbers. Even with the large "brain drain" from Hong Kong, Taiwan, and South Korea during the past two decades, the number remaining of university-educated or, perhaps more to the point, the number of educated from universities with high standards would dwarf those in most other developing countries.

It should next be noted that the list of names of economic successes is very similar to that of the list of major recipients of American economic and military aid. South Korea and Taiwan have received massive amounts of assistance, and Thailand and the Philippines have not been far behind (although the form of payments to the Philippines has been rather different from that of the other three). Even Singapore and Hong Kong are not really exceptions to this pattern. Both have been recipients of large inflows of Chinese capital from all over Asia, and Singapore, in addition, has benefited economically from large British military payments for main-

tenance of bases on the island. Only Malaysia is an exception
to the pattern. Although the beneficiary of some economic
aid, overall the country has probably been a net exporter of
capital.

Among the comparatively stagnant economies, both Burma
and Cambodia have often gone so far as to spurn assistance.
Indonesia has obtained large sums, although in per capita
terms far less than South Korea or Taiwan, but most of these
funds until after the 1965 coup were used for military
hardware and other unproductive activities.

It would seem, therefore, that U.S. aid has been a major
element in the recent economic successes of the region.
Correlations of this kind, however, can be deceptive. Rapid
growth in both South Korea and Taiwan did not really begin
until economic assistance was being cut back or, in the case
of Taiwan, phased out of existence altogether. Recent aid
payments to Thailand have in large part simply been used to
build up that country's already adequate foreign exchange
reserves. Still it is probably fair to say that U.S. assistance
was crucial in overcoming key barriers, in Korea the recovery
from wartime devastation and in Taiwan the problem of
financing both domestic capital formation and a huge army.
Once the economies really began to move, however, it was
domestic entrepreneurs and domestic sources of capital that
played the central role.

A third feature of growth in the region has been the role
played by exports. Since World War II most developing
countries have attempted to promote industrialization by a
policy of import substitution, that is, by placing high tariffs
and quotas on any import which could reasonably (or unrea-
sonably) be expected to be produced domestically. The result
has often been rapid growth for a time followed by stagnation as these industries hit against the ceiling of domestic
demand and, because of tariff-supported high costs, were

unable to compete on the international market. By way of contrast, Singapore and Hong Kong have achieved their high levels of performance without any significant tariff protection at all. Hong Kong's exports have been growing at rates usually well above 10 percent a year for two decades. It is common to dismiss the relevance of this record either because Hong Kong is not a nation-state or because, as an entrepot, it was peculiarly well suited to exploit export opportunities. But South Korea and Taiwan are demonstrating that one does not have to have been an entrepot to expand industrial exports. In South Korea, for example, exports in 1970 were more than seven times the level of 1964 only six years earlier. In Taiwan not only did overall exports rise rapidly, but manufactured exports increased from negligible levels to a point where they accounted for half of the overall total.

In one respect these developments in South Korea, Taiwan, and the two entrepots lead one to optimistic expectations concerning the economic future of these countries. They have built efficient industries that can compete with any in the world, and there is no reason to think they cannot continue to do so indefinitely. But there is a cloud over these prospects, and it concerns the question of whether these countries will be allowed into international markets. For reasons that will become apparent, the appearance of this cloud is of direct relevance to the policies of the United States and Japan, and hence its source will be discussed at length.

Economic growth, for all of its many benefits, always exacts a price, and the experience of the Asian nations in the 1960's and early 1970's was no exception. Perhaps the most dangerous element of the development of the 1960's was that large portions of the populations of many of the countries involved did not benefit much or at all from the process. This has been the case for a time with all nations that have industrialized, but there is reason to believe that the process has been particularly pronounced in recent years in Asia.

The problems arising out of inequalities in the distribution of income in Asia and the nature of the inequalities themselves have taken many forms. One part of the problem has been that growth has been mainly concentrated in urban areas. Agriculture, particularly the subsistence agricultural sector, has gained at a much slower pace and in some cases not at all. Rural poverty in turn has encouraged a mass exodus from the farms into the teeming slums of the major urban centers, an exodus that has commonly been far larger than the urban demand for the services of these individuals. Rapid rates of growth of the rural population have greatly accentuated the problem. High level urban unemployment has been endemic even in the presence of record increases in GNP.

Lack of good data tends to obscure the presence of the problem (except to one who lives in or even visits the principal cities of the area). An extreme example is Korea where farm output growth has been slow and where the farm population has fallen to less than half of the total, while Seoul has ballooned to a population of over four million (just under 15 percent of the population of the whole country). High birth rates among Malay rice farmers have swamped Malaysian government efforts to raise their incomes, and the situation is made much worse by the prevalence of high levels of insecure tenancy. The result has been migration to the cities where, barring government employment, most live on the margin of the urban economy. The situation in Indonesia appears to be even worse.

The political impact of the distribution problem tends to be particularly virulent where those who benefit from growth and those who do not are of differing ethnic or cultural backgrounds. It is probably no accident that most of the economic development in the region has been carried out by Chinese or by the one people closest culturally to the Chinese, namely the Koreans. Taiwan, Hong Kong, and Singapore are obvious cases in point. Economic growth in Malaysia has been largely confined to the Chinese community, and in Thailand Bangkok would seem to be the major beneficiary, and Bangkok is ethnically still in large part Chinese. The Philippines may have been the one exception.

Where Chinese are the major or only group to participate in the development of the modern sector, growth not only does not necessarily contribute to political stability, it may undermine it. Under such circumstances, it can become politically popular to attack and restrict the Chinese (or Indian) community even at the price of a markedly slower rate of increase in national product. Sentiments of this kind have had more than a little to do with the recent economic history of Burma and Indonesia, and they have been an important component of Philippine and to an increasing degree Malaysian economic policy.

There are numerous other kinds of inequalities of income distribution which are a source of difficulty. Regional income disparities within a given country, for example, are a constant problem. But the remaining one that has the most significance for the parts of Asia with which we are concerned, is the traditional one of the rich versus the poor. There are no figures, but there is every reason to believe that there are wide disparities in income in all the countries of the region. What is probably more important from the point of view of its political impact is that industrialization has made a number of individuals extremely wealthy. The good fortune of these businessmen has not gone unnoticed. Where it has at least in part resulted from collusion between officials and private entrepreneurs over the allocation of such things as import quotas, the reputation of the government has been seriously tarnished. Even where such is not the case, conspicuous wealth particularly when combined with conspicuous consumption has some and often many adverse consequences. These observations are not very original, but they tend to be forgotten by those overly fascinated with percentage increases in GNP. The Ayub Khan government of Pakistan fell at least in part because it ignored these issues, and they contributed to the downfall of the Malayan Chinese Association in the 1969 Malaysian elections.

This emphasis on problems of the unequal distribution of income, however, is not a preamble to a call for abandonment of the emphasis on growth. Historical experience suggests that most members of any given society are materially far better off in the long run in a society if they concentrate on increasing the size of the pie rather than on cutting up the existing one more evenly. There are, to be sure, those who argue that even substantial increases in real income for an individual leave him worse off if he still has only half or say a fifth of what his neighbors have, but that is to give envy an extraordinarily high place in the lexicon of human values, although it undoubtedly describes accurately what determines the political attitudes of some.

The point instead is that there are usually alternative paths to development, some with a higher political cost than others. Even where there are no alternatives, a country growing at 9 or 10 percent a year can well afford to sacrifice some growth in order to accomplish other important goals. Today, many of the countries of Asia are pursuing economic policies not unlike those followed by Japan in the decades prior to Pearl Harbor. Japan in that period enjoyed a rapid pace of industrialization, but one that was very unequally distributed. The farm sector was nearly stagnant, while the urban rich became richer. Like Korea, Taiwan, and Indonesia, to name the most conspicuous examples, Japan spent a substantial proportion of her wealth on armaments.

There are, of course, differences between Asian economic policies today and those of Japan before the war. An important one from the point of view of this discussion is the recent enthusiasm for foreign investment in most of the states of the region. Japan has generally kept foreign investors at arm's length. But the key difference between Japan then and the others now lies in the political sphere. Japan's political institutions were by any standards unusually strong and yet ultimately even they were unable to adequately control the pressures of rural poverty which contributed so much to the military adventures of the 1930's and 1940's. The political institutions of the Asian states with which we are concerned in this study, in contrast, are generally weak, although their vulnerability to upset varies considerably from country to country.

Thus the smaller states of East and Southeast Asia, which together have a population of some 300 million, have in many cases achieved a high degree of economic success but at considerable political risk. The concern of much of the remainder of this essay is whether there are steps which the United States and Japan either separately or together can take to promote continued economic growth in the region and to reduce the political risks. Before undertaking that task, however, a brief analysis of how the economy of the People's Republic of China, by far the largest economy in the region outside Japan, fits into this discussion.

CHINA AS A CASE APART

Although China's per capita income today is below that of the more rapidly developing states of Asia, when one multiplies this income by over 800 million people, one arrives at a total national income or product figure of around U.S. $100 billion or more. During the 1960's the rate of increase of Chinese GNP was slowed first by the aftereffects of the Great Leap Forward and then by the Cultural Revolution. Still, in spite of these setbacks, there was growth in per capita income in the 1960's and the rate accelerated in the early 1970's with the end of the Cultural Revolution. Barring future political upheavals, growth rates of 6 to 8 percent a year over a sustained period are not only possible but likely. China's economic performance, therefore, is likely to match that of some of the more rapid developers elsewhere in Asia. Why then do we not include it in the analysis of the effects of Japanese and American policies in the region?

The principal answer to this question is that Japanese and American economic policies will have little effect on what happens to the Chinese economy over the next decade and more, and the Chinese economy itself will not have much effect on economic development elsewhere in the region. China, for example, does not now allow foreign private investment and is not likely to do so anytime in the near future, at least not in large amounts. Nor is China likely to become a major recipient of foreign aid or high levels of long term foreign credits. In fact, since the early 1960's, China has been a net aid giver at levels in the early 1970's that have reached U.S. $600 million a year. China, of course, will accept credits for a few years at a time to overcome some temporary foreign exchange bottlenecks, but the money is likely to be obtained on commercial terms and in amounts that will put little strain on lending institutions.

The major reason why Japanese and American economic policies will have little effect on China, however, results from the fact that China has pursued an import substitution strategy with a vengeance. Where the other rapid developers of Asia have vigorously promoted exports and an expanding share of trade in national product, China has reduced its already small foreign trade share ($X+M$/GNP) from 7 to 11 percent (in the 1950's) to less than 5 percent in the early 1970's. There are many reasons for this Chinese emphasis on self-reliance ranging from a belief in it for its own sake to its relevance for an effective national defense posture. For these reasons it is unlikely that China will reverse this emphasis on self-reliance anytime soon. Chinese foreign trade will probably continue to grow, but the dollar value of that trade today is similar in size to that of many quite small Asian states and that is likely to remain the case as long as the trade of these smaller nations continues to grow as rapidly as in the past.

As will be argued below, several of the export oriented countries of Asia are in some danger of seeing foreign markets for their products stagnate or grow at too slow a pace to maintain the kind of overall economic performance that characterized these countries in the 1960's. That is not China's problem. All evidence for China points to the fact that it is not the availability of markets, but domestic production difficulties in the export sectors together with a lack of any commitment to export expansion that have hampered Chinese export development. Thus whatever the attitude of the United States and Japan toward increasing imports, China is likely to face few difficulties marketing whatever products it is willing and able to make available to the export sector, at least for the immediate future.

It is also improbable that relations between the United States and Japan (and others) will become poisoned by rivalry over the China market. Chinese imports have yet to pass through the U.S. $3 billion level and China, for political-military reasons if no other, is unlikely to give any one nation more than about 30 percent of that trade. Thus one can foresee a time a few years from now when Japanese exports to China might reach U.S. $2.0 billion and those of the United States perhaps U.S. $1.0 million, but for only a portion of this trade, perhaps a few hundred million dollars, will there be any real competition between the United States and Japan. Such sums will seem large to individual companies but small to governments concerned with multibillion dollar balance of payments surpluses and deficits.

THE ROLE OF ECONOMIC AND TECHNICAL ASSISTANCE

Even when the People's Republic of China is treated as a case apart, any discussion of the role of Japan and the United States in the economic, political, and social development of the rest of East and Southeast Asia should begin by noting that that role will be a secondary one. Leaving aside the question of external security, many of the most important issues are beyond the power of any outside nation to influence significantly. To take one important example, any attempt to apply external pressure on say Indonesia or Malaysia to carry out land reform is bound to fail unless such pressure is thought by the leaders of those governments to be in their own best interests. The issue is too vital to the futures of too many people within the country concerned for promises of increased assistance (or cutbacks) or a "better image" with the American and Japanese publics to have any influence. Most other major political reforms as well come under the heading of measures not readily subject to outside influence.

If the United States and Japan are to play an important role in these areas, it will probably mainly be through the long and uncertain route of helping train and educate the leadership elements in these societies. The problem is not one of winning "friends" for America or Japan, it is having individuals who can help make their societies run more effectively. The effects of past efforts in this area are often forgotten or disparaged, but a good many of the ablest and most reform-minded people with influence in the region received a part or all of their higher education in the United States or Britain. To mention only one of the more dramatic examples, where would Indonesian economic policy be today if it were not for the decision of a handful of members of the Faculty of Economics of the University of Indonesia to go abroad for advanced training and the fact that the means for doing so were available. It would be unfortunate if the present trends in attitudes of Americans toward the outside world were to reduce materially the publicly and privately sponsored possibilities in this area. It is to be hoped that control over these programs will prove to be too decentralized to be seriously damaged by declining governmental and foundation interest. The efforts of Japan in this area to date have been modest; and it remains to be seen whether that most formidable of obstacles, the language barrier, can be overcome.

If there are limits on what the United States and Japan can do to help, economic assistance still has a vital role to play at least in several Asian nations—but not all. China's lack of interest in aid has already been mentioned. As indicated above, Malaysia, Singapore, Taiwan, and Thailand have either never received much assistance or no longer require it. South Korea is increasingly able to finance its imports with export earnings and commercial credits although government to government low interest loans for several more years will smooth the transition to independence from foreign assistance.

Those most in need of continued aid are the nations of Indochina and Bangladesh. With the possible exception of Vietnam (North and South) these states are likely to require large amounts of assistance for a long period of time if they are ever to get to a stage of self-sustaining growth. Aid to these nations will also have to be in the form of grants or, what amounts to almost the same thing, given the weakness of their currencies, soft loans. The alternative of hard loans at 5 or 6 percent interest is likely to burden a country such as Bangladesh with heavy repayment costs a decade or two hence just as its economy is beginning to make real progress. Cambodia would be a similar case if the war there ever ends.

The one other nation in the region that has required large amounts of economic assistance is Indonesia. Barring another political upheaval there in the near future, however, aid to Indonesia is not the seemingly endless proposition that it now appears to be in Bangladesh. The rapid development of Indonesia's rich natural resources now underway and the recent rise in the prices of these resources should place the country in a position to pay for its imports on a commercial basis within a few years, if not sooner. Thus Indonesia may require more aid, but for only a short period of time. Under such circumstances hard loans at moderate rates of interest are not an unbearable burden and have the advantage of putting pressure on the Indonesians to use the money effectively.

Given Indonesia's weak administrative capacities, however, an interest rate will not by itself guarantee the efficient use of aid. In fact one important way in which Japan and the United States can contribute to Indonesian economic development will be to help design projects that can be protected from some of the less favorable aspects of the current Indonesian political scene. Japan's past experience with reparations payments to Indonesia, payments that were made with few questions asked or supervision given, illustrates how wasteful so-called "aid without strings" can be when the recipient's project design and administrative capacities are weak.

One way of accomplishing effective aid supervision without the high risks of political friction between aid giver and recipient is to channel that aid through such international agencies as the World Bank and the Asian Development Bank. In fact such international agency lending accompanied by careful supervision can be useful even in countries that are not short of foreign exchange but are short of means of protecting their modern enterprises from domestic political predators (this advice has, for example, been used successfully in Thailand). An important disadvantage of the international agencies is the difficulties they have in concentrating their efforts on a few strategic (from the point of view of development) countries in contrast to spreading their activities thinly across many nations. Thus there continues to be a role for bilateral United States and Japanese aid in places such as Indonesia even though such aid carries with it the danger of deeper political entanglements and resentments between donor and recipient.

PRIVATE INVESTMENT

Political dangers similar to those arising from the misuse of aid are even more apparent with private foreign investment. During the past several years many of the countries in the region have been going to considerable lengths to attract large American, European, and Japanese investors. It is as if all the popular political slogans about the evils of foreign economic imperialism had been forgotten. But it is unlikely that they will remain forgotten for long. The activities of Japanese private investors in Thailand and Indonesia, for example, have already generated adverse comment.

In some parts of the region, to be sure, foreign private investment does not pose much of a threat to domestic political stability. Hong Kong is an obvious case and Taiwan will probably continue to welcome foreign corporations as symbols of at least some form of international relations. South Korea's anti-foreign and particularly its anti-Japanese nationalism may be ameliorated as long as many Koreans feel a need to maintain a foreign presence as protection from an attack from the north. South Korea has also kept some control over the situation by limiting foreign direct investment and turning instead to loans that do not involve as much foreign control of domestic enterprises.

The real problem area is Indonesia and to a lesser degree Thailand. Unlike other countries in the region, Indonesia may have to depend on foreign private investors to an important degree. The one great hope for Indonesian exports and hence for freedom from dependence on foreign aid is through the development of its petroleum and mining resources. And this development, for a variety of reasons, mainly will have to be carried out by foreign firms. Thus, the country most vulnerable politically to the issue of "imperialism" is also the most dependent for its economic future and even its economic independence on the classic form of economic imperialism, the foreign exploitation of her mineral resources.Thailand is less dependent on foreign investment than Indonesia is likely to become, but Thai sensitivities to excessive foreign involvement, always high, are reinforced by a strong potential challenge from the political left.

Because such countries as Indonesia can benefit enormously from foreign private investment, it is clearly not a solution for American and Japanese policy makers to discourage such investment by their own nationals. Nor would policies designed to limit American and Japanese investment in Asia be feasible given the current competitive scramble among the world's developed nations for reliable sources of energy and other natural resources.

American and Japanese officials can, however, take steps to reduce the political impact of investment by foreign corporations. An important component in less developed nations' fear of Japanese and American investors is the belief that the power of these companies is great enough to threaten their basic sovereignty. In principle they can tell these corporations what to do, but in practice, if they try, they know that they may precipitate an international crisis, boycotts of their products, and the like. It is natural, of course, for individual corporations to defend themselves, but there are good reasons why the governments of the United States and Japan should avoid getting entangled in these quarrels. Government involvement strongly reinforces the belief that the battle is one between national independence and colonial dominance, and when the battle is fought on such terms, the usual results are substantial losses for both sides. Chile is the latest example of this process at work in the United States' relations with Latin America. There are numerous similar examples of greater or lesser virulence.

The way to avoid such confrontations is to make it clear that the power of the United States and Japan does not stand behind American and Japanese owned corporations operating in Asia. Repeal of the Hickenlooper amendment which requires foreign governments to compensate Americans whose property has been confiscated (or face loss of aid) would be one symbolic step in the right direction. Avoidance of statements and representations by American and Japanese officials and diplomats in support of investments abroad by their nationals might also help. On the positive side, Japanese and American willingness to make loans available to Asian states wishing to buy out strategic foreign owned enterprises would clearly indicate our sensitivity to the problem.

One should be under no illusions about how easy it will be to bring about this change in posture in either the United

States or Japan. Corporations have their own interest and the ability to make their views felt within their respective governments and some of these corporations, particularly ones looking for quick profits, will find the above suggestions inimical to these interests. It is also often difficult to separate investment and trade promotion. Export promotion has long been considered an important and desirable function of embassies, for example, and it is not realistic or even desirable to eliminate or reduce this role. Still there is a substantial difference between what is possible in the way of change and the current practices of the American and Japanese governments.

Failure to change will probably prove costly to both the United States and Japan, but more to the latter than the former. For reasons that are far from obvious, Asians appear to be more sensitive to the dangers of Japanese than American private investment. Although Japanese investment in Asia is rising very rapidly, it is still significantly smaller than that of the United States. Nor, in spite of the size of Japanese trade with the region, is Asia unusually dependent on Japanese products or Japanese markets. Raw material shortages make for a seller's market and Japanese manufactures can be bought elsewhere (at a higher cost to be sure).

The behavior of Japanese companies and company personnel is sometimes blamed for Japan's increasingly bad image in Asia. They are said to be too quick to resort to bribery and tend to be poor at communicating with local residents, preferring to live apart. But Americans (and Europeans) have often behaved in much the same way.

One suspects that the real reason why Japanese investors are currently receiving the brunt of criticism is that they are seen as the opening wedge in a Japanese attempt to establish hegemony over much of Asia. It is unlikely that the Japanese government is seriously contemplating such an effort and it is even less likely that such an effort would succeed. The point, however, is that many Asians believe the opposite to be the case. And a major reason why they hold this belief is because Japan, more than any other powerful nation, has made its economic expansion the center of its government's activities abroad and in recent years this has included the vigorous promotion of Japanese private investment. Indonesian and Thai demonstrations are only the tip of an iceberg of potential hostility. It is hoped that a repeat of the United States experience with Latin America can be avoided, but prospects at the moment are mixed.

TRADE POLICY

The vital question of trade policy remains. As indicated previously, a number of countries in Southeast and East Asia have come to depend heavily on the export of manufactured products, particularly textiles. The economic health of these nations depends on finding markets for their goods that are not only sufficient to maintain existing levels of exports but will allow for considerable expansion as well. During the past two years, however, there has been rising political pressure in America for increasing restrictions on such imports. If those attempting to impose these restrictions meet with success, the cautious optimism that now prevails concerning the economic health of South Korea, Taiwan, and Singapore will evaporate. The social problems and inequities that exist half hidden today will come to dominate the scene.

But the United States cannot be the only provider of markets for Asian manufacturers. Japan, by all economic logic should already be an importer of cheap factory products including textiles from its close neighbors. In practice Japanese restrictions have been so tight that imports from such nearby industrializing countries as South Korea, Taiwan, and Singapore have been held to a minimum, while exports to those same countries have soared. This picture is often obscured by the fact that Japan does import substantial amounts from some nations in the region, such as Indonesia, but such imports are mainly in the form of raw materials. Markets for countries not rich in raw materials have benefited much less from the Japanese economic boom of the past two decades.

The Japanese-American trade battles of the past two years have had both good and bad effects on the prospects for the export of Asian manufacturers. American efforts to restrict textiles has, of course, been an important item on the negative side. Japanese trade liberalization which increasingly appears to be real liberalization and not a public relations effort, is beginning to have a positive impact. Between 1969 and 1972, for example, Japanese imports from Taiwan have more than doubled although exports to Taiwan remain nearly three times as large.

The biggest impact of recent events on Asian trade in manufactures, however, has come from the revaluation of the Japanese yen. The impact is likely to be greater in markets outside Japan than in those within the country. South Korea, for example, has changed the value of the won with the dollar and hence has sharply devalued vis-à-vis the yen. Korea's textile industry, temporarily depressed by American moves, is hence once again booming with the prospect of cutting into Japan's nearly billion dollar textile export trade with Southeast Asia.

What is disturbing about the way in which Japanese-American trade differences have been resolved during the past two years is not, therefore, that these moves severely damaged the rest of Asia's economic prospects—on balance these countries may have gained at least for the moment. The problem is that the impact on the rest of Asia was often not even seriously considered prior to taking these steps. If the result had been a severe recession in South Korea instead of a boom, it is likely that few in Japan or the United States would have noticed until that recession with all of its political as well as economic implications was well underway.

There is no mechanical solution to this tendency of major economic powers to ignore the trade interests of smaller Asian economies. An Asian or Pacific common market is not realistic given the enormous political, economic, and even social differences between countries in the region. The only effective way to deal with the problem is to appoint men to carry out Japanese-American trade negotiations who are aware of the broader implications of their decisions and to give them sufficient political backing so they can act accordingly. It goes without saying that the secondary effects on Asia of Japanese-American trade decisions are most apt to be positive if both countries are moving toward freer trade either separately or together.

CONCLUSION

A theme of this essay has been that the United States and Japan will continue to be involved and have interests in Southeast and East Asia, and in particular that the stability of the region is likely to be a concern for some time to come. Implicit in the discussion has also been the belief that this involvement will continue whatever happens over the next few years in Indochina.

Also running through the analysis has been the view that Japan and America's major contribution to the promotion of stability and progress in the region will be in the economic sphere. Much of the above analysis would have to be fundamentally changed if the present gradual American military pullback were stopped or reversed.

Even a few years ago one might have argued with some justification that a nation whose influence was confined largely to the economic sphere in Asia was a nation likely to have little influence over the course of events in the region. A decade of rapid growth and the passing of Sukarno and his policies, both foreign and domestic, has greatly altered or should have altered the pessimistic views of the early and mid-1960's. The fast pace of industrial development by all appearances has contributed to stability in nations as disparate as South Korea and Singapore. But this growth is still fragile, and its contributions to political and social harmony over the longer run far from assured. Some aspects of the development process as it is being carried out in Asia, in fact, are exacerbating ethnic, regional, and class divisions and hence undermining stability.

The key elements in any "solution" to the sources of internal instability in the countries of the area will be such measures as land reform, a better balance in rural-urban priorities, increasing participation by various groups in the political process, and the like. The influence of Japan and the United States over these fundamental issues will be marginal at best. But whatever the outcome vis-à-vis such policies, there is little doubt that progress in these areas will not be assisted by ending economic development. In fact, only with fairly rapid growth will there be funds available to pay for many of the necessary social reforms.

Thus, it is clearly in the interests of both the United States and Japan to do what they can to make it possible for the performance of the 1960's and early 1970's to continue or, in the case of Indonesia, Bangladesh, and others, to improve. And it is also apparent that there is a good deal which the two countries can do to influence the economic future of the region either for better or for worse. Economic aid is still crucial at least to such nations as Bangladesh and for a time to Indonesia and South Korea, and the sums involved are well within the range of what Japan and the United States can be expected to have available for such purposes. Japanese and American private investment can also play a useful role if it can be promoted without sowing the seeds of future political turmoil. Over the long run, however, trade policy is likely to be far more important to the economic future of the nations of East and Southeast Asia (excluding China) than either aid or private investment.

Policy making in all these areas is greatly exacerbated by the very pace of change in Asia. The world has no long term experience with growth as rapid as that currently underway in much of Asia. We tend to forget, for example, that it was not until 1969 that Japan recorded its first balance of trade surplus since World War II and yet, within less than two years, alarmists were talking about the crisis created by this supposedly "permanent" competitive advantage. How much more complicated are relations when half a dozen countries and more are growing at 8 to 10 percent a year?

Given the pace of change, this essay cannot spell out in detail the specific measures necessary to accomplish our respective goals. New measures are continually being called for and old ones becoming obsolete. There are, however, common themes underlying these specific policies that are of lasting significance. It is these that have been emphasized here.

7

FUJI KAMIYA

Summit Talks in

Retrospect

During the generation since the Pacific war, Japan and the United States have witnessed several events marking major turning points in their mutual relations. In the course of these events, Japan has moved from a feudal to an independent relationship with the United States.

The first major event was, of course, the conclusion of the San Francisco Peace Treaty, signed in September 1951 and made effective in April 1952. From Japan's defeat in 1945 to the signing of the treaty, the U.S.-Japanese relationship had been similar to that between a shogunate and a *tenryo*, a territory controlled directly by the shogun in the Tokugawa period. Japan had no diplomatic relations with the United States; communications were accomplished through "liaison" offices.

Conclusion of the Peace Treaty elevated Japan from tenryo status to a position of *fudai*, in which a lord receives direct protection from the shogun but retains command of his own local hereditary territory. No longer was the United States a ruler directly governing Japan, but mutual relations between the two countries remained close, as symbolized by the U.S.-Japanese Security Treaty, which had been concluded with, and almost as part of, the Peace Treaty. The fudai not only relied almost entirely on the shogunate for its security but also had to seek the shogun's protection and assistance to meet the problem of achieving economic self-reliance. Hence Japan had no option but to remain a loyal follower, and it virtually abandoned any idea of an independent approach to national security. In that sense, Japan was almost in a state of isolation. This relationship inevitably bred, in Japan's posture toward the United States, an attitude of *amae* or taking U.S. protection for granted.

THE PILGRIMAGE

The second event was the emergence of the Kishi government in 1957. Nobusuke Kishi, arrested by GHQ as a class-A war criminal suspect immediately after the surrender documents were signed in September 1945, spent three years and three months in Sugamo prison. The very fact that he was nominated premier in 1957 marked a new step beyond the formal recognition of peace and the termination of the occupation. Japan had begun to leave the postwar era behind.

The Kishi government initiated a period of "pilgrimages" to Washington reminiscent of *sankin-kotai,* under which local samurai lords were obliged to pay regular visits to, and remain virtually as hostages in, the Edo castle of the shogunate in feudal days. In June 1957 five months after assuming the post of premier, Kishi called on President Dwight Eisenhower in Washington, D.C. This set an example which was to be followed by his successors as one of the major tasks and ritual chores they could hardly afford to ignore. The list of pilgrimages includes:

June 1957	Kishi—Eisenhower
June 1961	Ikeda—Kennedy

January 1965	Sato–Johnson
November 1967	Sato–Johnson
November 1969	Sato–Nixon
October 1970	Sato–Nixon
January 1972	Sato–Nixon
August–September 1972	Tanaka–Nixon[1]

With the exception of the last two, these visits were all cases of sankin-kotai. By using this label, I do not mean to emphasize Japan's subordinate position vis-à-vis the United States but rather to point to the fact that Japan's inherent position was increasingly recognized within a few years after the Peace Treaty. As a tenryo, completely subordinate to the shogunate, Japan had been denied even the privilege of sankin-kotai. Now that it had become a fudai, it was qualified to pay a visit to Washington.

It should be noted that Kishi was not the first Japanese premier to visit the United States after Japan regained independence. In 1954 Shigeru Yoshida toured Europe and stopped in the United States to confer with President Dwight Eisenhower and Secretary of State John Foster Dulles. However, the joint communique that resulted from this conference in November 1954 reflected graphically the fact that Japan was still living in a postwar politico- psychological environment. It stressed a superficial relationship of independence and equality by declaring that "their governments would, in cooperation with the free nations of Asia, continue their united efforts to maintain and promote the peace and prosperity of Asia." And it revealed a protector-protege relationship: "By various means since the end of the war the United States has been able to contribute substantially to the economic progress which Japan had achieved. The United States is aware of the efforts which Japan is making to solve its difficult economic problems and will continue to examine sympathetically means whereby it can assist the Japanese people to advance their well-being."[2]

Press commentators in Japan tended to judge the results of the premier's visit to the United States on the basis of the "souvenir" he had brought back from Washington.[3] Even Hayato Ikeda, then secretary general of the Liberal Democratic Party, commented that "the joint communique itself is a splendid souvenir."[4] Thus Yoshida's overseas tour was essentially a round of courtesy calls designed to express appreciation for Japan's readmittance to the international community.

In the years after 1955 Japan witnessed major internal and external events that led to a gradual departure from the postwar era: the Socialist party was united and the conservative parties were amalgamated (in 1955), Japan-Soviet relations were restored and Japan joined the UN (in 1956). Kishi's pilgrimage to Washington in 1957 was not an accident but a result of these events. "Before his departure for the U.S.," a Japanese newspaper wrote, "the premier explained to reporters that the significance of his scheduled tour lies in the fact that it was not so much for solving individual outstanding problems as for deepening mutual understanding of top leaders of the two nations through exchanges of their frank views."[5] American newspapers in Washington, however, seemed to be "wondering what views the premier would exchange with U.S. leaders . . . when the purpose of his visit is not so clear."[6] What seemed to escape the American press was the fact that Kishi's visit was to mark the beginning of a dialogue between the leaders of the two nations on basic diplomatic issues, a dialogue in which Japan was to be treated as a full-fledged partner.

The contents of the communique resulting from this meeting implied that Japan reaffirmed and accepted the anti-Communist policies of the United States without question.[7] At the same time, the communique clause referring to the Security Treaty reflected an understanding that the pact was essentially "transitional" and an agreement that the two governments would set up a committee to review it. This was a striking contrast to the flat denial Secretary Dulles had given Foreign Minister Mamoru Shigemitsu when he asked for a treaty revision during a visit to the United States in 1955.

The communique also pointed out that the two leaders "reviewed the great changes which have taken place in Japan in recent years, including Japan's extensive economic recovery and admission to the United Nations, both of which the President warmly welcomed." Observers noted in these words a new emphasis for U.S.-Japanese relations and began to use phrases such as "new era for Japan and the United States" or "new era of equality" between the two nations. Even a game of golf between Kishi and Eisenhower was called an "Eisenhowerish ceremony" designed to impress the public of the "new era."

Some elements of the new era were found in the fact that the communique made implicit reference to differences between the two countries on the question of China, as well as explicit reference to Japan's strong desire for the return of Okinawa. It was reported that in eleven items submitted by Japan for consideration by the United States in preparation for the communique was an item that allegedly said, "The administrative rights over Okinawa shall be returned to Japan in ten years."[8] However, the President, while reaffirming Japan's residual sovereignty, pointed out that "so long as the conditions of threat and tension exist in the Far East the United States will find it necessary to continue the present status." After the release of the communique, Kishi stressed the need for reversion but frankly confessed, "The U.S. side is not now in a position to let it go. Practically speaking, a partial reversion of the administrative rights cannot spell an end of the military administration." And he added, "Nor can we say confidently that Okinawa would be better off if it were returned to Japan."[9]

As a prelude to the revision of the Security Treaty, the communique revealed an agreement on the establishment of an "intergovernmental committee to study problems arising in relation to the Security Treaty." The United States also "welcomed Japan's plans for the buildup of her defense forces," as it was preparing to reduce its own forces in Japan, "including a prompt withdrawal of all United States ground combat forces."

Although Japanese demands appear to have been incorporated into the communique in a limited fashion, Kishi nevertheless expressed his appreciation for the fact that "both President Eisenhower and Secretary of State Dulles, as well as other U.S. leaders, lent their ears to his words," and he said he was convinced that a firm and lasting partnership had been established between the two nations.

EQUAL PARTNERSHIP

The next round of the U.S.-Japanese summit talks was held in June 1961 when Prime Minister Hayato Ikeda conferred with President Kennedy. The Security Treaty had been revised in 1960, followed by a series of riotous troubles in Japan that finally led to Kishi's resignation. The Ikeda cabinet that succeeded Kishi's emphasized a new political style of "low posture" and an economic rationale of income doubling, designed to boost public morale and to lay the cornerstone for the projection of Japanese economic growth on the international scene. As Professor Edwin Reischauer has described it, the Ikeda cabinet marked the beginning of "an ever lengthening period of calmer sailing—calmer in fact than anything Japan had experienced in many a decade."[10] Only four months after Ikeda assumed the premiership, the LDP faced a general election and won more seats than in the previous election of 1958.[11]

The struggle over ratification of the Security Treaty in 1960 had essentially been a manifestation of anti-U.S. nationalism, although it was not destined to lead to the denial of the treaty itself. What had begun as an anti-pact campaign ended as an anti-Kishi campaign, and with the ouster of Kishi, the public momentum subsided rapidly and the treaty's ratification was accepted. The psychological state of the Japanese people at that time was such that they were hesitant to let the new treaty come into effect without putting up some resistance, even though they recognized the need for the treaty and appreciated most of the improvements that had been incorporated in the revised treaty. Although this national state of mind was somewhat irrational, it reflected the delicate nationalistic climate that was beginning to emerge as the postwar psychology faded. The United States was merely the most readily available target for the new Japanese nationalism.

Thus as Japan, the fudai, increasingly gained confidence in her security and prosperity, it simultaneously appreciated and resented the existence of the shogun. The more secure—and accordingly, the more prosperous—Japan became, the stronger the resentment of the United States grew under the surface. Indeed, this is perhaps the Achilles' heel of any bilateral security arrangement. It was, at least, a contradiction that the Japanese faced for the first time in the fallout from the 1960 anti-pact explosion.

Premier Ikeda waited about a year for public sentiment to settle down before he made his pilgrimage to Washington. On the international scene, President Kennedy was looking for solutions to the Berlin problem, the proposed nuclear test ban, and possible approaches to detente with the Soviet

Union. China had improved its standing in the international community to the point where possible entry into the United Nations was becoming an issue. And Laos was a powder keg. Kennedy was thus concerned with cementing U.S. ties to Japan and reconfirming the basic views of the U.S.-Japanese security relationship. The Ikeda—Kennedy conference had significance for both leaders in their search for new approaches to international relations. Basically, they were both anxious to deepen mutual understanding and accomplish a more frank exchange of views.

Although Kennedy's personal gestures to Ikeda during his stay in Washington were calculated to demonstrate his high estimation of Japan's importance, the conference itself focused on global issues and the communique, with one or two minor exceptions, contained nothing but abstract expressions.[12]   Ikeda, who was concerned not to provoke the United States in the wake of the anti-pact riots, refrained from requesting the reversion of the Okinawa and Ogasawara islands, although the discussion did produce joint U.S.-Japanese cooperation to "enhance the welfare and well-being of the inhabitants of the Ryukyus." China, on the other hand, was a major issue in the conference and Ikeda revealed his views frankly, confirming the importance of Taiwan to the free world but reportedly emphasizing the limitations of the U.S. formula for blocking China's entry to the United Nations.[13] The communique said simply that the two leaders had examined "various problems relating to Communist China."

Generally speaking, the Ikeda—Kennedy summit was most significant in its contribution to a frank and candid exchange of views between Japan and the United States and in establishing the fact of Japan's importance to the United States. It thus served to remove the sense of apprehension about the future of U.S.-Japanese relations that had been created by the Japanese reaction to the revision of the Security Treaty. In a press conference held after the summit, the Japanese premier said, "In fact, I was surprised in attending this conference at the fact that the U.S. administration values Japan's importance more highly than I had so far imagined. President Kennedy and I became real friends."[14]

The two nations had confirmed their cooperative relationship under which they would pursue new avenues of foreign policy, while maintaining close contact as "mutual consultants." The new era had been replaced by the era of "equal partnership." Japan had finally freed herself of an occupation-postwar mentality in the glow of economic prosperity, and the United States had begun to realize the need to respond in kind to Japan's new status.

Nevertheless, the Japanese government failed to understand thoroughly why the basic thrust of the Kennedy administration was still directed to Europe first. If Japan had been able to look ahead, it might have seen that the United States would seek to revise its China policy once detente with the Soviet Union had been established. Instead, it continued to place its faith in what seemed to be a status quo U.S. policy toward Japan and Asia. Domestically, Japan was preoccupied with intensive economic growth and doubling national income, but psychological attitudes were growing as intensively as the economy. Against the background of a complacent political climate, Japan was beginning to acquire self-confidence as a big power. Through the decade of the 1960's Japan's sense of "big power" status continued to grow as her GNP rose to the third largest in the world.

AUTONOMOUS DIPLOMACY

Premier Eisaku Sato and President Lyndon Johnson met twice. The first meeting, in January 1965, came two months after Sato had taken office and established his intention to pursue a course of diplomatic action substantially different from his predecessor. President Johnson had just won a resounding election victory and was eager to replace the Kennedy era, to which he had dedicated himself after the assassination of President Kennedy, with a new Johnson era.

Major factors on the international scene had also shifted substantially between the Ikeda–Kennedy and Sato–Johnson summit meetings. Detente had begun to replace the cold war between the United States and the Soviet Union, the cold war having peaked with the Cuban missile crisis of 1962. The stabilization created by U.S.-Soviet detente, in turn, was leading to a more fluid state of international affairs, in which, for example, France and China were beginning to pursue policies substantially independent of their former protector-partners. Multipolarity was replacing bipolarity as the most popular word in international politics. The Sino-Soviet dispute was intensifying, and France was moving away from NATO, especially after its recognition of China in January, 1964.

The focus of world politics was gradually moving from Europe to Asia, where the situation was becoming increasingly critical. China had conducted her first nuclear test in October 1964 just as Khrushchev had been ousted from power in the Soviet Union. The United States had begun a major offensive in Vietnam after the Gulf of Tonkin incident of August 1964 had given President Johnson the excuse to retaliate against aggression, and American predictions of terminating the war by the end of 1965 began to fade. The situation that prevailed toward the end of 1964 was so critical that the United States faced the option of accepting the collapse of the South Vietnamese government or turning the Vietnam conflict into an American war.

These new international developments forced all the large

powers to reassess their own national interests. In Japan, the rising voices of "autonomous diplomacy" could be heard in and out of government, among both pro- and anti-U.S. groups, and the words "national interest" gained popularity.

It was against this background that Sato and Johnson met in January 1965, and the agenda of the meeting reflected their concern for the world situation. While previous U.S.-Japanese summit meetings had focused only on U.S.-Japanese relations—considering "petitions and requests" from Japan and concluding with customary agreements on U.S.-Japanese cooperation—the first Sato—Johnson meeting dealt with the basic issue of Communist China and the situation in Southeast Asia, as well as a wide spectrum of international security. Furthermore, Sato, throughout the negotiations, maintained his posture of "autonomous diplomacy," a political slogan to which he had committed himself early in his term.

Several points in the joint communique of this 1965 meeting gave evidence to the success of Sato's autonomous diplomacy.[15]   On the China issue, for instance, the two leaders expressed in parallel their different views: "The President emphasized the United States policy of firm support for the Republic of China and his grave concern that Communist China's militant policies and expansionist pressures against its neighbors endanger the peace of Asia. The Prime Minister stated that it is the fundamental policy of the Japanese Government to maintain friendly ties based on the regular diplomatic relationship with the Government of the Republic of China and at the same time to continue to promote private contact which is being maintained with the Chinese mainland in such matters as trade on the basis of the principle of separation of political matters from economic matters." The United States had earlier accepted, though informally, the principle of the separation of political and economic matters, as it had been expounded by Japanese leaders. However, the reference to it in the 1965 communique was proof that Japan's autonomy had been formally recognized, particularly when it is read against the reference to China in the 1961 communique, which merely pointed out the "examination of various problems" relating to China.

On basic Asian policy there was a sharp contrast between the 1961 and 1965 communiques. The former stated that: "The President and the Prime Minister expressed their concern over the unstable aspects of the situation in Asia and agreed to hold close consultations in the future with a view to discovering the ways and means by which stability and well-being might be achieved in that area." The 1965 communique, on the other hand, said that the two leaders: "recognized that the elevation of living standards and the advancement of social welfare are essential for the political stability of developing nations throughout the world and agreed to strengthen their economic cooperation with such countries." They also agreed to "continue to consult on the forms of such assistance" and the premier expressed a "particular interest in expanding Japan's role in developmental and technical assistance for Asia." This was the first time the two governments had explicitly recognized Japan's role in helping Asian nations develop and build a basis for political stability.

On the question of Okinawa, the joint communique revealed some signs that the U.S. position was beginning to move. Although it still contained much of the customary language on the importance of the Ryukyu bases to the security of the Far East, for the first time account was taken of the Japanese position on reversion: "The Prime Minister expressed the desire that, as soon as feasible, the administrative control over these islands will be restored to Japan and also a deep interest in the expansion of the autonomy of the inhabitants of the Ryukyus and in further promoting their welfare." The communique also made reference to some practical proposals aimed at reversionist sentiment, such as a plan to "broaden the functions of the existing Japan-United States Consultative Committee" and permission for former Ogasawara islanders to visit their ancestors' graves. Thus the new communique unlike its predecessors, was material evidence that the United States had begun to change its basic concept and was making the promise of reversion more explicit to the Japanese lest U.S. occupation of Okinawa be allowed to undermine the partnership.

Finally, on U.S.-Japanese relations in general, the communique stated: "The President reaffirmed the United States determination to abide by its commitment under the Treaty to defend Japan against any armed attack from outside." And the two leaders, in seeking common objectives, agreed that "the two countries should maintain the closest contact and consultation not only on problems lying between them but on problems affecting Asia and the world in general."

Following, publication of the communique, Secretary of State Dean Rusk commented that the communique opened a "new chapter" in U.S.-Japanese relations, words that became the new catch-phrase for this stage of the development of Japan's position vis-à-vis the United States. True, one might argue, there still existed a trace of the shogunate-fudai relationship in that the United States reaffirmed her obligations to Japan under the security pact, reflecting perhaps concern over the latest Chinese nuclear test.[16] Nevertheless, the communique did express quite clearly that Japan's national interest did not always coincide directly with that of the United States. The communique further indicated a trend in the U.S. government toward greater expectations that Japan should assume broader responsibilities commensurate with her increased national potential. In other words, the United States was expressing the inevitability of greater Japanese autonomy or a shift from fudai to *tozama,* a status in which a lord assumes independent financial and security responsibility but remains loyal to the shogunate. The price for greater independence would be a larger contribution to the shogunate system.

The results of the 1965 summit conference, however, were not so highly valued in Japan as they seemed to be in the United States. An *Asahi shimbun* editorial of January 15, for example, claimed that the communique presented "nothing fresh and new." Japanese correspondents stationed in Washington, on the other hand, tended to reflect the optimism that prevailed in the United States. An *Asahi* report from Washington, published on January 15, 1965, stated that "Everything went smoothly—far better than originally expected, depending on how you look at it. In fact, the premier had a hard time keeping a poker face as he successfully inserted almost all that he wanted."

FROM FUDAI TO TOZAMA

As is evident from the previous discussion, U.S.-Japanese relations were relatively uneventful and stable until 1965, with very few exceptions. In general the United States took the leading role in developing the relationship, taking initiatives that were presented to Japan in a relatively unprovocative fashion. Even during the 1960 anti-pact movement, Japan's breach of international protocol through de facto cancellation of the scheduled presidential visit left no lasting scar on the relationship. Sato's pilgrimage to Washington in January 1965, however, marked the end of the honeymoon, as it was followed by a series of discordant tones on both sides of the Pacific.

The first cause of disturbance occurred on February 7,

1965, when the United States began bombing North Vietnam, turning the conflict into full-scale war. This event
triggered in Japan—and throughout the world—a wave of
criticism of the U.S. presence in Vietnam and the nature of
her commitment to Asia. Even such doves as George Ball and
Edwin Reischauer were still confident enough of the Ameri-
canization of the Vietnam war to refute Japanese newspaper
accounts of the war.[17] In October 1965 Reischauer, then
ambassador to Japan, reacted particularly strongly to the
dispatches from Hanoi of Minoru Omori, a *Mainichi shimbun*
reporter.[18] The gist of Reischauer's statement was that the
Japanese talk about pacifism as a psychological reaction to
their Pacific war experience but think about peace only in a
negative, passive context of noninvolvement. Thus they show
little understanding of the U.S. engagement in Vietnam.
Americans, on the other hand, he stated, felt that they had
been dragged into two world wars precisely because they had
remained aloof from world problems. America, therefore,
could not accept the idea that the passive attitude of the
Japanese was a viable means to realize peace in Asia. If
Southeast Asia succumbed to communism, he maintained,
Japan would be most seriously affected because she depended on that area for one third of her trade. If Japan was
realistic about the consequences of this prospect for her basic
national interest, he questioned, how could she remain a
disinterested observer, indulging herself in criticism of the
United States?

Reischauer's countercriticism related not only to Vietnam
but to a larger sense of American dissatisfaction with Japan's
unilateral reliance on the United States along with the pacifist
stance of a disinterested observer of Asian security problems.
But a mutual sense of alienation was growing on both sides,
evidenced by the increasing frequency with which Japanese

commentators expressed serious apprehension about the future of U.S.-Japanese relations.[19]

The mounting tension between the two countries arose not only from the Vietnam war but from larger fundamental factors, namely, the Japanese inclination toward autonomous diplomacy and increasing economic self-confidence.[20] As the Japanese economy had been growing at a rate of 15.9 percent a year during the 1960's, U.S. economic growth had remained at 6.7 percent.[21] The discrepancies became painfully conspicuous in the second half of the 1960's. Furthermore, Japan's traditionally negative trade balance with the United States was beginning to shift the other way.

Finally, in 1965 Sato began to raise Okinawa as a policy issue. In August 1965, while visiting Okinawa, he made his now famous statement, "So long as Okinawa does not return to its homeland, Japan's postwar period will never be over. . . . This is the heartfelt feeling of all Japanese people."[22] The Okinawa reversion issue now escalated into a major political objective of the Sato cabinet, an obsession that was to remain with Sato for his entire eight years of office.

Nobusuke Kishi had taken the initiative to liberate Japan from her postwar environment; his younger brother Eisaku Sato—on the strength of Hatoyama's successful diplomacy with the Soviet Union and Ikeda's emphasis on economic growth—strove to expedite and complete the implementation of his brother's initiatives. He saw Okinawa as his main diplomatic target for establishing once and for all Japan's total sovereignty in the international community. Recognizing the value of Ikeda's economic rationalism, he kept the ball rolling, but he did not feel that economic achievement alone was sufficient for Japan in its new age. Material accomplishments, he believed, had to be accompanied by what he

called "mind" (spiritual) achievement. This required "autonomous diplomacy," "autonomous defense," and above all,
the reversion of Okinawa.[23] In short, Prime Minister Sato set
out on a course of meshing international economic expansion
with nationalistic political achievement.

In time the Okinawa issue ignited a powder keg called
neonationalism and created complex, difficult problems in
postwar Japan where nationalism and anti-Americanism were
inherent and obvious. While Sato originally hoped to solve
the Okinawa issue within the framework of U.S.-Japanese
friendship, he was inevitably faced with recurrent phenomena
that ran counter to his true intention. As the issue developed,
it became clear that post-Okinawa U.S.-Japanese relations
would be substantially different than those of the postwar
years.[24]

It was against the background of these circumstances that
the Sato—Johnson communique of November 1967 was produced. Euphemistically speaking, the process of development
that occurred between the 1965 Sato—Johnson meeting and
that of 1967 was analogous to Japan's transformation from
the position of fudai to tozama—an ambitious undertaking
that held the bright prospect of achieving the third largest
GNP in the world.

Sato's departure for Washington in 1967 triggered a chain
of anti-American outbursts throughout Japan. The day before he left, an elderly man committed self-immolation in
front of the premier's official residence; as Sato departed
from Haneda airport, riot police were fighting bloody battles
with a few thousand radical students in the near vicinity. [25]
Nationwide public concern for Sato's trip ran high and was
expressed openly as never before, because it was generally
believed that the success or failure of the Okinawa issue
hinged on this summit meeting, regardless of whatever security problems might be outstanding in Asia.

Public opinion may have been emotional, but the Japanese government had yet to develop a rational policy for the return of Okinawa, based on objective analyses of Asian and American concerns. In fact, there had been no program whatsoever in 1965 when Sato visited Okinawa or in 1966 when it was argued that educational administration should be returned separately from other forms of administration, or even in 1967 when total and complete reversion had become a consensus. The pressure of public opinion had outdistanced the Japanese government to the point where it had to call for reversion without a concrete program. It had only a "blank sheet of paper" on which a definitive policy was yet to be written.

The U.S. government, on the other hand, was hardly in a position to promise the reversion of Okinawa while involvement in Vietnam was at its height. Neither was President Johnson in a position to make a promise on Okinawa reversion that would have to be carried out by whatever administration succeeded his in 1968. In full knowledge of these circumstances, the Sato government nevertheless proceeded with its "bad timing" in an attempt to head off the potential danger it faced from the mounting anti-American nationalism in Japan. Public opinion had reached new heights of emotionalism when Sato flew to Washington in November 1967.

And indeed, the main feature of the 1967 joint communique was the new language on Okinawa that it incorporated:

[The Prime Minister] further emphasized that an agreement should be reached between the two governments within a few years on a date satisfactory to them for the reversion of these Islands. The President stated that he fully understands the desire of the Japanese people for the reversion of these Islands. At the same time, the President and the Prime Minister recognized that the U.S. military bases on these islands continue to play a vital role in assuring the security of Japan and other free nations in the Far East.

As a result of their discussion, the President and the Prime Minister agreed that the two Governments should keep under joint and continuous review the status of the Ryukyu Islands, guided by the aim of returning administrative rights over these Islands to Japan and in the light of these discussions.[26]

The communique also included an agreement on the early reversion of the Ogasawara Islands and the establishment of a new tripartite committee (U.S.–Japan–Okinawa) to plan for the reversion of Okinawa.

Despite the notable advances toward Okinawa reversion that had been made in the course of this meeting, reactions in Japan were decidedly equivocal. In general, the favorable Japanese reactions were that the communique marked a step forward in the solution of the Okinawa reversion issue, despite the fact that it had been raised at an inauspicious time and negotiated in the midst of several unfavorable circumstances, such as China, Vietnam, and the upcoming U.S. presidential election. Critics of the communique focused on its reflection of the two leaders' views of China and Vietnam. They felt that Sato had made too many concessions to Asian security in return for very little progress on the reversion of Okinawa, particularly in appearing to support the U.S. bombing of North Vietnam by stating that "reciprocal action should be expected of Hanoi for a cessation of the bombings." Missing from the communique, argued the critics, was Japan's "autonomous" posture that had been manifest in the 1965 Sato–Johnson communique.

NIXON DOCTRINE AND OKINAWA REVERSION

When the joint communique of 1967 was released, commentators in Japan began a heated exchange as to whether the phrase "within a few years" in the English text really meant "two to three years," as it had been officially trans-

sion to the climate of resurgent nationalism that prevailed throughout Japan, from Hokkaido to Kyushu.[27]

The United States, at the same time, had elected a Republican president and the Nixon Doctrine was already being articulated. This concept, as it was introduced in Nixon's press conference on Guam in mid-1969, was not exclusively the invention of either Nixon or the Republican Party.[28] A determination by the United States that its military commitment in Asia had to be modified had already been reflected in President Johnson's 1968 decisions for a partial halt (in March) and total halt (in October) of bombing operations across the 17th parallel. By 1969 there was a sense of national consensus for a reduction of the U.S. security commitment in the world.

However, the United States was vague about the dimensions of its "disengagement" from Asia, except that Japan was to play a somewhat larger role. Some were criticizing Japan for taking a "free ride" on U.S. security guarantees and not sharing the burden, even financially. Nixon himself, before his presidential election, appeared to have considered a stronger security role for Japan. One thing was certain: the Nixon Doctrine was not meant to remove the United States as a Pacific power. Therefore, it was natural that a stable alliance with Japan become an even more compelling argument for the U.S. government. This indeed was the factor that led inevitably to the 1969 agreement on the early reversion of Okinawa in return for Japanese recognition of the military value of the U.S. bases on Okinawa. At the same time, the United States government had finally reached the conclusion that nuclear weapons would have to be removed before Okinawa returned to Japan, thus the major question that had been left hanging between the summit meetings of 1967 and 1969 had been resolved.

The 1969 communique read: "As a result of their discussion, it was agreed that the mutual security interests of the United States and Japan could be accommodated within arrangements for the return of the administrative rights over Okinawa to Japan."[29] To accomplish this, the "two governments would immediately enter into consultations regarding specific arrangements" to expedite reversion during 1972. Paragraph 8 of the communique further stated that "The Prime Minister described in detail the particular sentiment of the Japanese people against nuclear weapons and the policy of the Japanese Government reflecting such sentiment. The President expressed his deep understanding and assured the Prime Minister that, without prejudice to the position of the United States Government with respect to the prior consultation system under the Treaty, . . . the reversion of Okinawa would be carried out in a manner consistent with the policy of the Japanese Government as described by the Prime Minister." Accordingly, a new interpretation was added to the meaning of "prior consultation" in the security treaty. Whereas the words had previously been understood as a Japanese right to veto major U.S. military moves in Japan, they now came to imply that the Japanese government would not necessarily veto major U.S. military moves. In other words, instead of just "no" it was now "yes" or "no". This related in particular to the Korea and Taiwan clauses that were inserted in the communique, in which Japan recognized the relationship between its own security and that of its two neighbors.

Thus, with the return of Okinawa, came a strong affirmation from the Japanese government of the security aspects of its alliance with the United States. The two leaders agreed that they "highly valued the role played by the Treaty . . . in maintaining the peace and security of the Far East including Japan and they affirmed the intention of the two governments firmly to maintain the treaty on the basis of mutual trust and common evaluation of the international situation." These references tended to mirror a subtle, unstable sense of equality between Japan, which was in the process of climbing the hill, and the United States, which was in the process of coming down the other side. This was the general tone of the communique, as the Japanese read it.

PARTNERSHIP WANES

The years 1971 and 1972 were eventful for U.S.-Japanese relations: Nixon's announcement of plans to visit Peking (the first Nixon shock); Nixon's announcement of import controls to defend the value of the dollar (the second Nixon shock); intergovernment agreements on textiles; devaluation of the dollar, revaluation of the yen; the U.S.-Japanese summit meeting at San Clemente: the Sino-American joint communique; the reversion of Okinawa; the U.S.-Japanese summit meeting in Honolulu; and the normalization of Sino-Japanese relations. The succession of these events brought Japan and the United States into the third phase of their postwar relationship.

The stresses that the relationship underwent in 1971 were triggered by the "Nixon shocks," or the suddenness for Japan of his major diplomatic moves. In part, because of Japan's unpreparedness, the shocks intensified frictions and antagonisms that had been building for some time. As President Nixon explained in 1972, "Some of our actions during the past year placed the Japanese Government in a difficult position . . . We regret [this] but could not do otherwise." What happened, in effect, "only accelerated an evolution in U.S.-Japanese relations that was, in any event, overdue, unavoidable, and, in the long run, desirable."[30] Japanese observers, however, refused to accept that the United States had had "no other alternative" to this surprise diplomacy. They believed that Nixon was making a deliberate attempt to force Japan to feel a sense of isolation and to reaffirm the importance of her relations with the United States, in particular "to reorganize Japan-U.S. relations in the direction of reciprocity."[31]

Since these events, Japan and the United States have made mutual attempts to control the mounting tension. Japan made concessions in textile negotiations and agreed to the U.S. position in the United Nations over the issue of Chinese representation. President Nixon flew to Anchorage to meet with the emperor on his way to Europe and, in a meeting with Prime Minister Sato at San Clemente, the President agreed to a one-year truce in the trade war. The United States also returned the administrative rights over Okinawa to Japan on schedule. Despite testimony from both sides that the worst differences between Japan and the United States had been settled, there remained the question of whether the aftereffects of the "Nixon shocks" in Japan had really passed so quickly. Nixon, himself, stated in his 1972 foreign policy message that the "process of adjustment will sometimes be arduous."

During the partnership period of the 1960's, the Japanese had spoken of equality and responsibility without actually freeing themselves from a psychological state of *amae*, common to a long relationship between a protector and protege. This long-standing state of mind was not to be dispelled easily, even in the 1970's. For example, in trade relations Japan was very slow to respond to American pressures to reduce the very large trade gap that had developed between the two countries, depending instead on the United States to somehow work it out herself. When the textile problem surfaced as the most critical issue between Japan and the United States in 1970, Japan made very clumsy responses for two and a half years, displaying unwarranted optimism in her relations with the United States. Japan's main failure in this case was not to interpret the political significance of the issue for President Nixon, who had made a commitment on textiles during his 1968 presidential campaign. To Japan it remained a purely economic matter and was allowed to escalate beyond control. At the same time, the Japanese public was viewing the government's position as autonomous diplomacy. As an *Asahi shimbun* editorial of June 24, 1970 stated: "The latest U.S.-Japanese textile talks were the first case where Japan refused a U.S. demand and the first time in postwar diplomatic history where Japan conducted her diplomacy autonomously."

Japan's autonomy-oriented posture toward the United States was basically a reflection of a curious mixture of nationalism, *amae,* frustration, and self-confidence. The "Nixon shocks" may in fact have been calculated slaps at this state of mind. However, whether they were or not, they did leave a deep scar on the U.S.-Japanese relationship that may never heal completely.

Between 1971 and 1972 the theory became popular in both Japan and the United States that the basic problems in the relationship were economic. The fact that the United States barely reacted to the Sino-Japanese joint communique of September 28, 1972, which was a clear-cut case of autonomous diplomacy on the part of Japan, tended to support this theory. Nevertheless, despite the heated exchanges over economic issues between the two countries, economic relations are still based on a fundamental complementarity between the two economies. Such complementarity does not seem to be present in political relations between Japan and the United States. What complementarity may exist in relation to the Security Treaty is not destined to remain for the indefinite future. Thus the basic issue for attention would appear to be political relations, including national psychology, public sentiment, and other more invisible factors.

As pointed out earlier, one destabilizing factor in U.S.-Japanese political relations has been the revival of nationalism in Japan. Furthermore, the Liberal Democratic Party has been losing its grip as the standard bearer of nationalism. It has for a long time appealed to the public on the basis of "national interests," as the custodian of national security and economic interests, as well as the cost accountant for both. As autonomy vis-à-vis the United States became a public goal, the LDP faced a dilemma, particularly in regard to its insistence on the maintenance of the U.S.-Japanese security system. While the party has been able to convince the public of the benefit to be gained from that relationship, this argument does not appeal to nationalism, a sentiment which tends to disregard benefit. The wider nationalistic sentiment has spread in Japan, the more support the LDP has lost. The party has been unable to appeal to the public on the basis of domestic issues and since 1972 has lacked popular diplomatic or foreign policy issues. With the anticipated intensification of pollution and inflation, the LDP is undoubtedly faced with a sort of instability and stagnation that it has never experienced.

If a clearly discernible threat to Japan existed, the rise of nationalism in Japan would probably have little effect on the Security Treaty. But the development of detente between the United States and the Soviet Union, the United States and China, and North and South Korea, has eliminated much of the threat that existed previously to justify the pact. It is true that the Chinese concern for the continuation of the treaty which became manifest in the course of the normalization of Sino-Japanese relations gave the pact new international significance. However, if the climate of detente and dialogue between former adversaries continues, the subtleties of this *raison d'être* for the Security Treaty are likely to escape the Japanese public, which will simply see the absence of any threat.

The recent emergence of China as a third party related to Japan's national interest also has added new dimensions to the U.S.-Japanese relationship. Both Japan and the United States must now view Asian affairs in a different context, and there are bound to be differences of interpretation on both sides. In this connection, it should be noted that the possible impact on Asia of the Sino-Japanese normalization of diplomatic relations does not seem to have been evaluated in quite the same way in the Honolulu and Peking communiques.[32] If the U.S.-Japanese relationship is to remain amiable, both must face squarely the problems inherent in the changes Asia has recently undergone.

Finally, the relationship is being further complicated by the vagueness that has been introduced with the "multipolarization" of world affairs. Can we afford to let the relationship slip into the muddy waters of such a fluid situation? Or can we somehow manage to salvage a strong U.S.-Japanese relationship and use that as the basis for Japan to stabilize its relations with the international community in general? Answers to these questions are the crux of the problem the two countries face today. We are standing at a crossroad where a new course of action must be charted for the future of all aspects of the relationship between Japan and the United States—political, security, and economic. The complacent partnership that existed in the 1960's must be replaced with a new concept.

8

TADAO ISHIKAWA

The Normalization of Sino-Japanese Relations

On September 29, 1972, the Sino-Japanese Joint Communique was signed and diplomatic relations between Japan and the Peoples' Republic of China were normalized. The process leading up to this event flowed quite rapidly because both sides seemed to favor the earliest possible conclusion. On the Japanese side, normalization of relations with China was at the top of Prime Minister Tanaka's list of diplomatic tasks. On the Chinese side, there was an unexpectedly prompt and highly positive response to the Japanese prime minister's posture.

THE CHINESE OVERTURE

Why did China change its attitude just as the Tanaka cabinet was being formed, while its stance on the normalization of relations had been consistently negative prior to the resignation of the Sato cabinet? There appear to have been five basic factors behind the change in the Chinese attitude.

1. Diplomatic posture. China's approach to international relations has undergone a dramatic change since the autumn of 1969. During the Cultural Revolution Chinese diplomatic posture was the product of an ideology: denunciation of American imperialism and Soviet revisionism provided the foundation for a diplomatic formula that was to unite those revolutionaries who could identify with these principles against the counterrevolution. This formula made it difficult for other countries to act in concert with China, because most countries maintain close diplomatic relations with either the United States or the Soviet Union.

With only slight exaggeration, it can be said that the result was the natural diplomatic isolation of China, with the estrangement of almost all countries except Albania and Tanzania. Furthermore, the denunciation of Soviet revisionism proved to be one of the decisive factors behind the three major Sino-Soviet border clashes in 1969. The Soviet military threat has been of prime concern to Chinese leaders since that time. Finally, as China emerged from its preoccupation with the Cultural Revolution, it began to see military potential in Japanese economic power, which had grown tremendously during the period of the Cultural Revolution.

All these conditions finally forced China to reexamine its diplomatic posture. Since ideology had failed to provide the foundation for diplomatic maneuverability, China was left to consider a diplomacy based on national interests. The new realistic diplomacy that evolved was, in short, a more power-political view of international relations. From this perspective, to have no diplomatic relations with Japan, one of the strongest nations in Asia, naturally appeared disadvantageous in light of China's own national aspirations. The restoration of diplomatic ties with Japan, therefore, began to assume an aspect of urgency.

It should also be noted that this change in diplomacy was prompted by the following factor. The power of the so-called extreme radicals of the Cultural Revolution, whose activities were strictly ideological, began to decline in 1968 and the leadership passed into the hands of Chou En-lai, who behaves more realistically, and the military leaders, who had great concern for the Soviet military threat.

2. Sino-Soviet relations. President Nixon's visit to the Soviet Union in May 1972 had the effect of increasing the Soviet threat to China. When the Soviet Union succeeded in gaining American support for a long-heralded European Security Conference, the threat in Europe began to diminish for the Soviet leadership. Soviet military forces deployed against the European threat could now be redeployed, which to the Chinese meant greater potential for a Soviet strike against China.

Furthermore, in the wake of Sino-American rapprochement, the Soviet Union approached Japan to negotiate a peace treaty, accepting the inclusion on the agenda of outstanding territorial problems. Foreign Minister Gromyko was promptly dispatched to Japan by way of emphasizing the seriousness of Soviet intentions to forge a closer friendship with Japan. The Soviet government's improvement of relations with Japan would have been a great disadvantage to Chinese foreign policy. Only the soonest possible normalization of diplomatic relations with Japan could have rescued the situation.

3. Termination of the war with Japan. From the Chinese standpoint the war had not yet been terminated with Japan. The weight of this factor in Chinese considerations of the advantages of normalizing diplomatic relations can only be a matter of conjecture, but it is probably safe to guess that, because of the significance of the war with Japan to the history of the Chinese revolution, those political leaders who themselves had participated in the war would also wish to participate in its termination. Furthermore, because normalization of diplomatic relations with Japan would, in some sense, settle the Taiwan problem, Chinese leaders would be

to normalize diplomatic relations and second by the use of elastic terms that allow each side to claim to have maintained its integrity.

A more detailed analysis of the communique reveals two major concerns: the settlement of problems surrounding the termination of the state of war; and future relations between Japan and China. The first issue required the solution of a number of basic questions: Japan's responsibility for the war, Chinese insistence on termination of the state of war, treatment of the "three principles for the restoration of diplomatic relations," and war reparations. The second issue involved the establishment of basic principles by which future Sino-Japanese relations would be guided and is as remarkable for what is not stated as for what is stated.

1. Responsibility for the war. The communique clearly states that "The Japanese side is keenly aware of Japan's responsibility for causing enormous damages in the past to the Chinese people through war and deeply reproaches itself." This is in fact the position expressed by the Japanese government since the era of Prime Minister Sato and it is likely that the Japanese side, without much qualification, had intended to insert these words in the communique long before the negotiations were arranged.

2. Chinese insistence on war termination. Japan and China are clearly divided on the question of "the termination of the state of war." Japan adheres to the validity of the Japan–Republic of China Peace Treaty, concluded when Japan recognized the government of the Republic of China as the sole legal Chinese government. Although the notes and agreed minutes accompanying that treaty make it quite unmistakable that its applicability is limited to Taiwan, the Pescadores, and all the territories which might thereafter come under the control of the government of the Republic of China, the treaty was nonetheless ratified by the Diet and successive cabinets have maintained publicly that the treaty is lawful and valid. The Japanese government could not reverse itself on this matter in 1972.

The Chinese government, on the other hand, has also maintained publicly that the Japan–Republic of China Peace Treaty is unlawful and invalid, and was equally unable to depart from this stand in 1972. Thus the question of war termination focused on the lawfulness and validity of the Japan–Republic of China Peace Treaty. From the Japanese standpoint, the state of war had been terminated when the peace treaty was ratified; from the Chinese standpoint, the state of war could be terminated only when diplomatic relations were established between Japan and the People's Republic of China.

The solution to this dilemma was political. An expression was adopted that could be adjusted to the claims of both sides according to necessity. The preface to the joint communique states that "The two peoples ardently wish to end the abnormal state of affairs that has hitherto existed between the two countries." The phrase "termination of the state of war" does not appear in this section. In the next sentence it is stated that "The termination of the state of war and the normalization of relations between China and Japan—the realization of such wishes of the two peoples—will open a new page in the annals of relations between the two countries." However, it should be noted that there is no specification as to the *time* of the termination of the state of war.

From the Chinese standpoint, therefore, it is possible to interpret the state of war to have been terminated when the "abnormal state of affairs" was ended. The Japanese side, on the other hand, can read that the state of war had already been terminated and that Sino-Japanese diplomatic relations were then normalized in order to "open a new page in the annals of relations between the two countries."

Thus Clause 1 reads: "The abnormal state of affairs which has hitherto existed between the People's Republic of China and Japan is declared terminated on the date of publication of this statement," but it is not stated that the state of war is terminated by publication of the joint communique in order to establish diplomatic relations. In sum, the Chinese side interprets the end of the "abnormal state of affairs" to mean the "termination of the state of war," while the Japanese side interprets the end of the "abnormal state of affairs" to mean the end of the hostile relation which existed even after the ratification of the Japan—Republic of China Peace Treaty that terminated the war.

3. *"Three principles for the restoration of diplomatic relations."* The preface to the joint communique states that "The Japanese side reaffirms its position that in seeking to realize the normalization of relations between Japan and China, it proceeds from the stand of fully understanding the three principles for the restoration of diplomatic relations put forward by the Government of the People's Republic of China. The Chinese side expresses its welcome for this." Clause 2 of the joint communique further states that "The Government of Japan recognizes the Government of the People's Republic of China as the sole legal Government of China," indicating Japan's full acceptance of the first principle for the restoration of diplomatic relations with Peking.

The Japanese position on the second principle, the question of the territorial sovereignty over Taiwan, is somewhat more equivocal. Clause 3 of the communique states that "The Government of the People's Republic of China reaffirms that Taiwan is an inalienable part of the territory of the People's Republic of China. The Government of Japan fully understands and respects this stand of the Government of China and adheres to its stand of complying with Article 8 of the Potsdam Proclamation." Terms implying Japanese recognition of the Chinese claim to territorial sovereignty over Taiwan appear to have been strenuously avoided. The words to "understand" (meaning to "take note") and to "respect" are used instead, on the assumption that the employment of both words, rather than only one of them, lends a stronger tone to the Sino-Japanese joint communique.

The phrase, "Article 8 of the Potsdam Proclamation,"[3] however, remains to be explained. The question is why there was only reference to Article 8 of the Potsdam Proclamation rather than a direct quote from the Cairo Declaration. I would guess that the Chinese side insisted on the quotation from the Cairo Declaration, but the Japanese side resisted and, in defending its position, finally agreed to adopt a reference to the Potsdam Declaration. Since the Cairo Declaration was drawn up by the leaders of the Allied Powers without Japanese participation, Japan is not legally responsible for its terms. On the other hand, Japan did agree to the Postdam Proclamation at the end of World War II. However, the terms of the Proclamation were decided by the Allied Powers and Japan merely accepted them. Thus, with regard to the Taiwan problem, Clause 3 of the joint communique can be interpreted to mean that Japan merely observes the decision made by the Allies and has no concern beyond that point. In substance, however, Clause 3 could also mean that Japan recognized the Taiwan problem to be a matter that should be dealt with by the Chinese. Obviously, the Chinese side did not succeed in bringing the Japanese side to use the word "recognize," but it may be said that the Peking government put an end to the question of territorial sovereignty over Taiwan by restating Japan's adherence to Article 8 of the Potsdam Proclamation, as well as the words "fully understand and respect."

The joint communique avoids altogether the third principle for the normalization of diplomatic relations, that is, the claim that the Japan—Republic of China Peace Treaty was unlawful, invalid, and to be renounced. Foreign Minister Masayoshi Ohira simply made a statement at a press conference to the effect that the normalization of diplomatic relations with the People's Republic of China obviated the reason for the existence of the Japan—Republic of China Peace Treaty. This was one way to announce the termination of the peace treaty. Here again, a compromise was reached to allow different interpretations for both sides according to their respective claims. The Japanese side was able to support its position that the treaty with Taiwan had been valid until the signing of the joint communique; the Chinese desire was met by the termination of Japanese diplomatic ties with Taiwan.

4. *War reparations.* Clause 5 of the joint communique deals with war reparations: "The Government of the People's Republic of China declares that in the interests of the friendship between the peoples of China and Japan, it renounces its demand for war indemnities from Japan." It should be noted that if, as the Chinese claim, the state of war had not been terminated until the date of the joint communique, the text should by logical necessity read: "It renounces its *right* to demand." If the joint communique had read thus, the Japanese claim to the lawfulness and validity of the Japan—Republic of China Peace Treaty would have been negated, because from the Japanese standpoint Chinese rights to demand indemnities were waived in that treaty.

FUTURE SINO-JAPANESE RELATIONS

The basis for future Sino-Japanese relations is laid in Clause 6 of the joint communique: the two governments "agree to establish durable relations of peace and friendship between the two countries on the basis of the principles of mutual respect for sovereignty and territorial integrity, mutual nonaggression, noninterference in each other's internal affairs, equality and mutual benefit and peaceful coexistence." And furthermore, "In keeping with the foregoing principles and the principles of the United Nations Charter, the governments of the two countries affirm that in their mutual relations, all disputes shall be settled by peaceful means without resorting to the use or threat of force." It is likely that both sides had no trouble agreeing on this language.

Clause 7, however, which elaborates on the matter, does leave some room for question. It happens that the statement in the clause that "Neither of the two countries should seek hegemony in the Asia–Pacific region and each country is opposed to efforts by any other country or group of countries to establish such hegemony" is identical with part of the text of the U.S.-China joint communique of February 1972. It is probable that the Chinese side insisted on its adoption. To preclude the possibility of that sentence being interpreted to mean that Japan and China would work together to oppose other countries seeking hegemony in Asia, the Japanese side probably insisted on the insertion of the clause, "The normalization of relations between China and Japan is not directed against third countries." This implies that neither country shall by any means alter its existing relations with third countries and that opposition to hegemony in Asia will not be carried out in the form of a Sino-Japanese alliance.

THE MISSING ISSUES

As mentioned earlier, the Sino-Japanese joint communique is also notable for what is missing from the text. First there is the question of the U.S.-Japanese Security Treaty. It is entirely likely that, had the Sino-Japanese negotiations been carried out two years earlier, the subject would have been discussed in the communique negotiations, because the Chinese side at that time appeared to credit the Security Treaty with promoting Japanese militarism. However, sometime before the communique negotiations, China almost ceased this line of argument. It is suspected that China began to view the existence of the security treaty system as a factor inhibiting the growth of Japanese militarism. Furthermore, the gradual withdrawal of American troops from Asia in accord with the Nixon Doctrine has reduced the threat of the Security Treaty to China. In addition, it is likely that the Chinese side understood the Japanese desire to restore diplomatic relations in accord with the San Francisco Peace Treaty system. Therefore, the question does not seem to have arisen in the communique negotiations.

The other important question that is missing from the text is the future of relations between Japan and Taiwan. The most logical interpretation of this is that the Chinese side tacitly accepted that Japan would wish to continue economic, cultural, and personnel exchanges with Taiwan in spite of the break in diplomatic relations.

THE ADVANTAGES OF NORMALIZATION

The Chinese side probably gained significant and tangible advantages from the normalization. In addition to the long-term benefits that will accrue to China's diplomatic posture, relations with the Soviet Union, and economic development, there were a number of immediate positive effects. First, the normalization improved Peking's international status. In the past Taiwan has been supported mainly by the United States and Japan. Now Japan recognizes Peking as the sole legal government of China and only maintains de facto relations with Taiwan. Thus, it may be said that the legality of the

Peking government has now become much less questionable and its international status has improved measurably with Japanese recognition.

Second, the communique represented a significant step in the direction of settling the Taiwan problem in favor of the Peking government. When the Sato–Nixon communique of November 1969 stated that "the maintenance of peace and security in the Taiwan area was also a most important factor for the security of Japan," it might have been expected that Japan should consider Taiwan as part of its life line. However, in September 1972 the Japanese side fully understood and respected the Chinese position with regard to Taiwan, viewing it as a matter that should be dealt with by the Chinese. This was a benefit to the Peking government.

Third, it is conjectured that normalization of Sino-Japanese relations has had considerable impact on the Southeast Asian countries and enhanced Chinese maneuverability in the region.

A final diplomatic benefit to be mentioned is the enhancement of Chinese opportunity for influence in Japan through diplomatic channels. China can now legally pursue those activities it considers necessary for the fulfillment of its national interests. This is important because Japan is undoubtedly a large factor in determining various aspects of China's future.

Domestically, the Sino-Japanese communique tended to increase the stability of the Chou En-lai leadership. To have succeeded in realizing the long-stated goal of normalizing relations with Japan, as well as making a significant step in the direction of settling the Taiwan problem, has enhanced Chou En-lai's position in the domestic political structure.

The Japanese benefits from the normalization are less tangible and immediate than those accruing to China. First, a possible gain may come from the opening of formal channels for negotiations between Japan and China. It is unlikely that the two countries always share common interests on all matters; rather, it is natural that friction will arise. Negotiations between the two governments are highly important in order to prevent minor frictions from erupting into strained situations. However, whether Japan's diplomatic position becomes in fact advantageous is contingent upon its basic diplomatic posture, especially toward the United States and the Soviet Union.

The possible enlargement of Japan's sphere of activity in international politics is an important result of the normalization for Japan. Because of the emergence of multipolar international situations, Japan can no longer completely depend on the United States, which now finds it more difficult to represent the interests of the Western world as a whole, and consequently Japan must become more self-reliant in the pursuit of its national interests through diplomacy. If Japan's diplomatic initiatives with China result in more reasonable diplomatic postures by the United States and the Soviet Union toward Japan, there may be additional benefits to be gained from the normalization with China. Caution would dictate, however, that if Japan were to enter into an alliance with China or even lean too heavily in that direction, it runs the risk of confrontation with the United States or the Soviet Union, resulting in possible deterioration of its maneuverability.

It is also of benefit to Japan that the normalization of relations with China increases the degree to which Chinese activities are regulated by the rules of international society. China, too, has become compelled to obey the rules and is expected, at least according to my own wishful thinking, to contribute to further stability in Asia. It is almost unnecessary to mention that the normalization indeed contributes to Japan's security.

Finally, there are important advantages in the normalization for Japanese domestic politics. After President Nixon's visit to China, opinions about the normalization of Sino-Japanese relations had become more and more divergent, even among the Liberal Democratic party members, causing political instability. The normalization, however, appears to have removed the cause of this instability in Japanese domestic politics.

THE DISADVANTAGES OF NORMALIZATION

There are few apparent disadvantages for China in the normalization of relations with Japan. It might, for example, intensify the Soviet Union's feelings of confrontation with China, it might reduce North Korea's and North Vietnam's confidence in China, it might make it more difficult for China to attack Soviet revisionism, or it might give those in China who disagree with Chou En-lai's leadership more reason for criticism. However, these problems would have arisen in any case with the Sino-American rapprochement of February 1972. The question is only to what degree they may have been aggravated by the Sino-Japanese normalization later in the year. I think the degree of aggravation is slight.

By contrast, the disadvantages of the normalization of relations for the Japanese side are slightly more apparent. First there are those that arise from breaking diplomatic ties with Taiwan. For example, inconveniences in trade and investment and difficulties in protection of Japanese residents in Taiwan are bound to appear. Second, it is conceivable that the Soviet Union, the United States, and the Southeast Asian countries entertain some unrest about the normalization of diplomatic relations between Japan and China. Although they have all welcomed the normalization formally, the Soviet Union has done so on condition that its own interests shall not be harmed, and the United States may have felt some concern about the possible consequences of the Sino-Japanese rapprochement on the U.S.-Japanese Security Treaty, in connection with the utility of U.S. bases in Japan for defense of Taiwan and the balance of power in Asia. The Southeast Asian countries may fear Japan's action in collaboration with China and they are concerned lest Japan lean too heavily toward China and lose interest in the region. Under such conditions, therefore, Japan's diplomatic maneuverability could be seriously hampered should Japan's commitment to China be excessive.

In sum, the gains to China from the normalization of diplomatic relations with Japan are highly practical and any losses could not be serious. For Japan, on the other hand, the possible gains are yet to be proved in the shaping of future relations between Japan and China, particularly in connection with U.S.-Japanese and Soviet-Japanese relations. Consequently, Japanese diplomacy, especially toward China, must henceforth be planned very cautiously.

9

DONALD C. HELLMANN

Japan and China:

Competitors in a Multipolar World?

The normalization of relations between Tokyo and Peking in the fall of 1972 symbolically marks the dawn of a new era in Japanese foreign policy. Relations with China have been in the center of the Japanese international horizon throughout the twentieth century, and the significance of this most recent diplomatic move is best perceived in the broader setting of contemporary global and regional affairs and in the context of Japanese politics since 1952. Indeed, an examination of the China problem during the past two decades from the perspective of Tokyo, inevitably leads to a consideration of the central features of Japan's foreign policy during this period: the dynamics of the foreign policy-making process, the evolution of policy goals, and the place of Japan in global and regional international affairs—especially her relations with the United States. The speed, drama, and importance of the recent agreement has led to an unfortunate emphasis on its immediate ramifications. However, the issues involved touch directly on both the fundamental assumptions of post-war Japanese foreign policy and the *modus operandi* of the international system, which perforce demand that a more comprehensive focus be employed. Before there can be mean-

leadership passed into the hands of Chou En-lai, who behaves more realistically, and the military leaders, who had great concern for the Soviet military threat.

2. Sino-Soviet relations. President Nixon's visit to the Soviet Union in May 1972 had the effect of increasing the Soviet threat to China. When the Soviet Union succeeded in gaining American support for a long-heralded European Security Conference, the threat in Europe began to diminish for the Soviet leadership. Soviet military forces deployed against the European threat could now be redeployed, which to the Chinese meant greater potential for a Soviet strike against China.

Furthermore, in the wake of Sino-American rapprochement, the Soviet Union approached Japan to negotiate a peace treaty, accepting the inclusion on the agenda of outstanding territorial problems. Foreign Minister Gromyko was promptly dispatched to Japan by way of emphasizing the seriousness of Soviet intentions to forge a closer friendship with Japan. The Soviet government's improvement of relations with Japan would have been a great disadvantage to Chinese foreign policy. Only the soonest possible normalization of diplomatic relations with Japan could have rescued the situation.

3. Termination of the war with Japan. From the Chinese standpoint the war had not yet been terminated with Japan. The weight of this factor in Chinese considerations of the advantages of normalizing diplomatic relations can only be a matter of conjecture, but it is probably safe to guess that, because of the significance of the war with Japan to the history of the Chinese revolution, those political leaders who themselves had participated in the war would also wish to participate in its termination. Furthermore, because normalization of diplomatic relations with Japan would, in some sense, settle the Taiwan problem, Chinese leaders would be able to "complete the eyes of the painted dragon" of the Chinese revolution.

The recurring leadership purges in China seem to have left a considerable gap in experience and ability between the first and second generation of revolutionary leaders and there is some question whether the first generation of Chinese leaders places full confidence in the second generation. At least we may conjecture that the first generation leaders would wish to handle the normalization of relations between China and Japan themselves. If they missed the opportunity with the Tanaka cabinet, they would have been compelled to wait several more years, an unattractive prospect for those who were mostly over seventy years old already.

According to unconfirmed information from some of those who made contact with one of the top Chinese leaders, Premier Chou En-lai reported that Lin Piao had opposed the Sino-American rapprochement, as well as the normalization of Sino-Japanese relations. Although this information is questionable in light of the past practice of the Chinese Communist party to lay all the blame on Lin Piao, it is nevertheless difficult to deny the possibility. If it is true, then the passing of Lin Piao from the scene would have truly made it easy to normalize diplomatic relations with Japan.

4. The Chinese Economy. Chinese economic construction cannot but have been a highly important factor in consideration of the normalization of diplomatic relations with Japan. The fact is known that China began to make a strenuous effort to develop its national economy in the autumn of 1969. Although the first ten years of Chinese economic development after the establishment of the Peoples' Republic were marked by great progress, the failure of the Great Leap Forward brought a sudden decline in production. The recovery experienced during Liu Shao-chi's so-called adjustment period was followed by the blow of the Cultural Revolution. By 1969 production had recovered to the level of 1966. Considering that the 1966 production level was only slightly higher than that of 1959, it would appear that hardly any economic growth was attained during the second decade of the new republic.

It is likely that the present Chinese leadership recognized that economic success contributes to increased stability in the leadership itself, as well as strengthening national power necessary for China's pursuit of international activities. While it is not presumed that China would forsake the principle of "self-reliance," international isolation is obviously not possible if economic growth is a serious goal. China must make use of foreign inputs to its economy, particularly advanced foreign technology, to stimulate the as yet underdeveloped Chinese technology. The normalization of relations with Japan would be highly advantageous in this connection.[1]

5. *Tactics.* There also seems to have been an important tactical reason for the Chinese decision. Because the Tanaka cabinet had declared that the normalization of Sino-Japanese relations was a top priority diplomatic task, a prompt and positive response by China could have the effect of driving Tanaka's government into a one-way alley. From the Chinese standpoint, therefore, it seems most likely that this was perhaps the decisive factor in the timing of the Chinese overtures for normalization.

With these factors, then, as the main pressures behind the Chinese decision, shortly after the resignation of the Sato cabinet and before the formation of the Tanaka cabinet, the Chinese government sent Hsiao Hsiang-ch'ien to Japan. The desire to begin negotiations for normalization with the incoming cabinet was expressed and preliminary arrangements were made for such negotiations to take place.

THE CONDITIONS OF THE JAPANESE RESPONSE

A sense of urgency on the Chinese side for normalizing relations with Japan enhanced the Japanese negotiating position, although not to the extent that Japan gained the obvious advantage. Japan was essentially in the same position as China in that its domestic politics required prompt normalization of relations with China. The Tanaka cabinet could not have retreated on the matter without risking a fierce attack from the opposition parties and the press in unison. Internal disorder within the Liberal Democratic party would also have been unavoidable.

The slogan of the Tanaka cabinet, "a government of decisions and actions," had awakened great public expectations. If normalization of relations with China, an avowed priority of the Tanaka government, had not been realized, the cabinet would have suffered severe blows in the coming general election.[2] Thus the Tanaka cabinet had little choice but to proceed with normalization.

With Japanese domestic politics creating this kind of pressure for the Tanaka cabinet, it could not have been in an advantageous negotiation position with China under any circumstances. However, the urgency of the Chinese overture did at least have the effect of improving the Japanese position to the point where it was nearly equal with that of China. Thus the negotiations for the joint communique demanded compromises from both sides in order to realize the shared goal of normalization. That this was true is clearly demonstrated in the joint communique itself.

THE TERMS OF THE JOINT COMMUNIQUE

The Sino-Japanese Joint Communique of September 29, 1972, is characterized first by basic agreement on both sides

ingful speculation concerning Japan's future relations with China and the implications for Japanese-American relations it is essential to clarify the basic assumptions and the legitimate parameters of the discussion. That is the subject of this chapter.

DEFINITION OF THE PROBLEM

The point of departure for discussing Japanese policy toward China must be the fundamental nature of the current multipolar order and the response of Washington and Peking to the new international realities. No region is more affected by the breakdown of the bipolar order than East Asia. One important but rarely noted implication has been the creation of a focus for international competition in which the two dominant regional powers, Japan and China, participate on a rough level of parity with the superpowers. Partly this has grown out of a reduction of the globalist priorities of the United States and the Soviet Union, changes ultimately rooted in the failure of their past policies in this region. Partly it is the result of the remarkable rise to international prominence of China (in the political-military area) and Japan (in economics), so that both nations now cast long, overlapping shadows of differing hue over the East Asian nations. More than any time since 1945, whether and how international conflict will be managed in East Asia is a matter of concern and uncertainty for both Tokyo and Peking.

Although the prospects for avoiding war in the region in the years immediately following settlement of the war in Indochina may be good, it is utterly quixotic to assume that this short-term relaxation of tensions is simply the first stage of a conflict-free international order (a "generation of peace"). A number of forces converge to produce deep instability in the region: the highly uncertain implications for international behavior of the profound economic and social changes occurring in all East Asian nations; the conflicts of interest tied to past and current national competition that are aggravated by ideological cleavages between communist and noncommunist political groups; the virtual impossibility of a "power balance" given the permeability of states to "people's wars" and the resistance of China to any attempt to freeze permanently the status quo; the failure of the superpowers to articulate their short-term or long-term objectives in Asia, far less to build effective alliance systems or to lay the foundations for neutralization of the region; and most important, the extreme uncertainty regarding the future policies of the status quo oriented Japanese and of the Chinese Communists. The two superpowers and the Chinese recognize that peace in Asia, even if achieved by diplomatic maneuver, ultimately depends on a "power balance" rooted in military force, and all see Japan as inevitably playing an expanded security role.[1] Under these conditions, it remains highly conjectural how Japan can continue to ignore the *modus operandi* of the prevailing international system while expanding her material interests abroad but defining her security narrowly in terms of territorial self-defense. Japan's often articulated policy of permanent military noninvolvement (an international "experiment unprecedented in world history"),[2] is limited by Tokyo's growing regional economic preeminence and the inherently unstable conditions in East Asia. Consequently, it is appropriate, indeed imperative, to envision China and Japan as direct and full competitors in East Asia.

The multipolar world is also characterized by nation-centered political and economic competition among the "great powers," which inevitably heightens the complexity and uncertainty of international relations. Calculations from the viewpoint of national self-interest underlay China's sudden willingness to normalize relations with Japan, and a similar emphasis is both implicitly and explicitly part of current American policy. President Nixon has repeatedly said, "We are not involved in the world because we have commitments; we have commitments because we are involved. Our interest must shape our commitments, rather than the other way around."[3] Thus, the certitude of the containment era has been replaced by what has aptly been labeled "indeterminacy,"[4] and under the concept of "realistic deterrence" there is an emphasis on more narrowly defined national security interests and a concomitant assumption that East Asian nations can and will assume fuller responsibility for their own defense. Similarly, whereas the United States saw economic relations with Japan until the late 1960's in terms of providing aid and markets to strengthen an ally and bring her into the club of industrialized non-Communist nations, now the image is that of a major national economic competitor against whom pressures must be brought to rectify serious bilateral (and global) trade and monetary imbalances. In the context of an increasingly nation-centered and indeterminate international order, the normalization of Sino-Japanese relations must be seen simply as an essential preface to a story yet to be told.

Despite the critical importance of these fundamental changes in the external milieu, domestic politics remains the filter through which all Japanese foreign policy must flow. If the broad shape of the China problem is defined for Tokyo by the external environment, its essential life and character is provided by the salient definition this issue receives in Japanese politics. This latter point will be subsequently elaborated, but here it is essential to make some prefatory remarks about the general limitations imposed on Japanese international behavior by the way foreign policies involving major *political* issues are made. This decision-making process proscribes bold leadership and virtually assures a passive and reactive role for Japan in international politics. The fragmented structure of the ruling conservative party, a style of authority that requires at least tacit consensus among all the responsible participants involved in decision-making (in this case party faction leaders), the extreme degree to which intraparty politics has been involved in all major foreign policy moves, and the deep policy and ideological cleavages with the opposition parties, have produced a kind of policy immobilism.[5] Barring an unexpected reversal of past trends altering the relative strength and modes of operation of the parties or the sudden emergence of a nationalistic consensus, this style of policy formulation will continue to restrain leadership no matter what the personalities or issues of the moment and ensure that Japan proceeds incrementally from one issue to another without a general strategic calculus.

There is a general recognition within Japan of the need for a new "independent" foreign policy, but there is no consensus on what the content of the policy should be. Part of the confusion grows out of uncertainty regarding the future shape of the international order, but the *Alice in Wonderland* quality of the internal policy debate will continue to impede the easy formulation of a new strategic posture. Foreign policy discussions among the conservatives have transpired mainly in private and in response to external (international) pressures and have been colored by intraparty factional considerations. Since 1950 the opposition Left and the media have been deeply absorbed in international affairs, but they have either rigidly clung to abstract moral positions (for example, anti-Americanism and an undifferentiated moral commitment to peace) or used specific issues to further their own political purposes. One consequence has been to give a curiously involuted focus to the foreign policy debate. The Japanese have moved from one concrete issue to another absorbed in short-term international goals and internal political tactics, avoiding to an extreme degree matters of *Real-politik* beyond the American alliance. Consequently, the foreign policy debate within Japan and actual developments in international politics have progressed on largely parallel planes. Given the domestic political system, it would be difficult to create a realistic debate regarding strategic alternatives, far less come to a consensus on a new set of policy goals. Indeed, what Japan will confront in the next few years is not just the choice of more appropriate new policies, but a challenge to the quasi-isolationist and pacifist assumptions underlying the policies of the last two decades—an ironic mirror image of the kind of challenge that the United States now faces. This lack of consensus together with the immobilist style of leadership creates a pattern of foreign policy making which is manifestly unsuited for the currently fluid international situation and for the frequent and rapid changes of direction that will be required for successful operation in an indeterminate multipolar world.

Before turning specifically to Japan's current relations with China and the attendant implications for the Japanese-American alliance, it is necessary to question to what extent Tokyo's foreign policy will be calculated ("rational") responses to the external environments. Virtually all commentaries on the nation's future international role presuppose that the Japanese policy makers will select the "appropriate" policy in terms of external realities and a given set of "values." A main thrust of this discussion is to suggest that this is not the case, and that Japanese institutions of decision making inhibit rapid, flexible response and produce reactive not active policies. The incapacity for bold leadership, the extremely politicized nature of the policy-making process, and the lack of a basic consensus, assure that Japanese policies will be largely derivative from the tangled web of domestic political forces. Moreover, the indeterminacy and complexity of the multipolar world render it improbable that Japan, or any nation, will for long manage international conflict through deft maneuvers by statesmen and professional diplomats. Contrary to the implicit assumptions of the Kissinger model of the international system, it seems highly unlikely that in the wake of the failure of the policies of the superpowers in East Asia (and the domestic political repercussions of these failures) a more tractable set of conditions will emerge. As the history of the twentieth century bears witness, the basic determinants of Asian international politics are compelling and impersonal forces rooted in conflicting national aspirations and interests beyond the full grasp of any country's policies. Consequently, in analyzing Japan's foreign policy in general or toward China in particular, emphasis should not be on a priori scenarios postulating a reversal of history or the moral imperatives of the peace constitution but rather on the complex and changing patterns of domestic and international politics which will continue to determine the direction of the nation's role in the world.

THE CHINA PROBLEM IN JAPANESE POLITICS

To a degree exceeded only by relations with the United States, the China problem has been central to the foreign policy debate in Japan. Extraordinary emotional and symbolic importance surrounds this matter for all politically articulate groups. China at once stands as a revolutionary, nuclear-armed Asian power directly competing with Japanese interests, as the critical key to war or peace in the region, as the world's largest untapped market, and as a nation with which cultural-historical connections are so profound as to cast an aura over things Chinese that transcends immediate political-economic conditions. That the China issue supercedes party lines is evident from the composition of the

groups that long led the campaign for normalization of relations with Peking—a motley coalition of nostalgic, conservative Sinophiles from the prewar era, opportunistic businessmen in search of the legendary China market, and left-wing
Maoist revolutionaries. Because of the salience and definition
this issue has within Japanese politics, adjustment of Tokyo's
external relations with Peking has been and will remain an
extremely complicated problem. Moreover, the intensity of
concern has tended to a definition of the China problem
narrowly in terms of Japan's relations with the two Chinese
governments (rather than in the context of Asian and global
affairs) and to an exaggeration of the capacity of the Japanese to affect the situation.

Until the United States moved in 1971 to establish more
cordial relations with Peking, Japanese policy toward China
was conducted on two distinct levels. With the right hand
they limited diplomatic recognition to the Nationalist government, sponsored the "important question" resolution in the
United Nations' General Assembly (thereby delaying Peking's
admission to the world organization), scrupulously adhered
to American sponsored trade restrictions, and cultivated extensive economic ties with Taiwan. With the left hand, the
Japanese, through various cultural, political, and economic
missions, established more varied and extensive contact with
the mainland than any non-Communist nation. The result
was a kind of de facto "two Chinas" policy, involving an
ostrich-like position regarding the uncomfortable political
and security issues raised by the growing international power
of Peking. This triangular relationship between Tokyo,
Taipei, and Peking graphically illustrates both the advantages
and inadequacies of the trading company philosophy underlying Japanese foreign policy. Although the Nationalists and
the Communists adamantly insisted that there was only one
China and that politics and economics are inseparable and

sporadically imposed restrictions against Japanese trade, Japan steadily expanded economic relations and became the leading trading partner of both countries. Then the spate of moves by other nations to recognize Peking commencing in late 1970, which culminated in China's admission to the United Nations and the visit of President Nixon to Peking, ultimately led to Japan's diplomatic recognition of China. However, the sudden resolution of an issue that had been so long avoided proved particularly divisive within the ruling conservative party.

Despite the seemingly dramatic reversal, of course, in a basic sense Japan still has a de facto "two Chinas" policy and many critical aspects of this issue are far from resolved. Attitudes rooted in the legacies of the fifty years of Japanese colonial rule over the island, together with strong anti-communist sentiments, and the extensive contacts cultivated since 1952 provide the basis for the "Taiwan lobby" within the Liberal Democratic party, a group which still holds a powerful intra-party position. Internationally, Japan's relations with Taiwan are integrally related to the security alliance with the United States in ways for which the recent recognition of Peking poses difficult problems. The U.S.-Japanese Mutual Security Treaty seeks to maintain through the use of U.S. bases in Japan the "international security of the Far East"—a commitment which clearly extends to Taiwan and directly contradicts the current "one China" posture formally supported by Tokyo. Moreover, Japan has made clear it hopes to maintain and expand the already extensive economic ties with the Taipei government. Until the status of Taiwan is more fully settled, it will remain a major stumbling block to the development of a viable and comprehensive Japanese policy toward East Asia.

Japan's posture toward China since 1952 graphically illustrates the generally immobilist character of the foreign policy-making process. If, until 1972, Japan's overall China policy was schizophrenic, regarding Peking it was prayerfully passive. Bilateral relations were determined almost entirely by responses to American diplomatic pressures or Chinese policies, or to the drift of world politics. China's criticisms of Japan were monotonously consistent and concentrated on opposition to the alliance with "American imperialism," collaboration with the "Taiwan bandits" and the "American puppet regime in South Korea" and in the late 1960's on the rise of "Japanese militarism." What ultimately initiated change in Tokyo–Peking relations was a policy shift by the Chinese combined with the alteration of the climate of world opinion to bring China more fully into international society and the pressure this trend placed on Japan to acquiesce. In recognizing Peking, Japan took no real initiative, achieved the goal of normalization by essentially accepting the terms of the other nation, and displayed once again a passive role in international affairs.

All Japanese political parties have been deeply touched by this question for some time. It was the issue of China policy that gave rise to policy factions within the Liberal Democrats in the mid-1960's, divisions which were encouraged by frequent "informal" visits of prominent party leaders to Peking and Taipei. Even though the Japanese will henceforth give priority to relations with the People's Republic of China, real consensus on this issue has yet to be achieved within the conservative party and it will be ensnared in future factional struggles for party control. The Socialists too have long made China policy an inter- and intra-party political football. There has been general agreement on the need to recognize the People's Republic of China, so the debate among themselves has centerd on how fully Maoism should be accepted and on the tactics for politically exploiting the issue within Japan. From the mid-1950's until the early 1970's it was popular

sport for Socialist leaders to visit Peking, ritualistically de-
nounce Japanese and American imperialism, and then have a
heated intraparty wrangle about the real meaning of the
words employed. In the short time since normalization, the
Socialists stumbled badly by bitterly attacking the "mili-
tarist" Fourth Defense Plan of the conservatives, only to have
it explicitly endorsed by the Chinese as "appropriate."[6] The
Japanese Communist Party has greatly improved its internal
unity and electoral strength since abandoning a pro-Chinese
position in the mid-1960's. However, now, when it is *de
rigeur* among the Left to support rapprochement with
Peking, the party is in the awkward position of being labeled
by the Chinese as one of the "great enemies" of the true
Communist revolution, and it was the only party to condemn
the U.S.-China move toward reconciliation as an "unprin-
cipled union." This prolonged interest in and the babel of
voices regarding an issue which has at best been ambiguously
resolved ensures that China policy will continue to be deeply
affected by internal events and will bedevil Japanese diplomacy over a wide range of issues.

In a basic sense, China and the United States hold unique
and competitive places in the Japanese political conscious-
ness. Both nations continuously draw extensive attention
from the mass media, the intellectuals, and the opposition
Left, which form the core of articulate public opinion in
Japan. An obsessively critical concern for America in the
media and the shrill and unbroken anti-American campaigns
by the political Left have ensured that every issue of the
alliance is accorded dramatic attention and has magnified the
salience of America's role in all areas of policy. At the same
time, the level of concern in this debate, both pro- and
anti-American, has centered not so much on concrete conflicts of interest as on the grand issues of peace and democ-
racy—matters of principle with strong emotional and ideo-

logical overlay. The United States has served as a kind of international referent for the Japanese,[7] and until recently, was annually overwhelmingly rated as the "most liked" country in public opinion polls. China has never had a comparable hold on the mass public (for example, one out of three Japanese in mid-1967 did not know that a Communist government controlled China), but among the politicians and the articulate public there has long been a deep-seated but ambivalent attraction to China. Within the opposition subculture, this attraction has been supplemented by deep-seated antipathy to the United States[8] and the strongly pro-Chinese mood created within Japan prior to normalization is an example of how those groups can influence foreign policymaking in an important way. In the immediate future, the rapidly expanding contacts with China together with continuing modifications in the American alliance will continue to keep relations with these two nations a touchstone of Japanese foreign policy. The hyper-concern regarding China and the United States will take on special significance if Japan does in fact become a regional "great power," for the appropriate sustaining mass mood will *pari passu* measure international autonomy and nationalism in terms of relations with both powers—with highly uncertain results.

SINO-JAPANESE EXTERNAL RELATIONS

A first look at security relations between Japan and China reveals a topsy-turvy world. The People's Republic is rapidly developing a fullscale nuclear arsenal; has one of the highest defense budgets in the world, measured as a ration of GNP; gives voice to revolutionary international aims; and has, directly or indirectly, participated in the two major East Asian wars since 1945. Japan has no nuclear weapons and the lowest rate of defense expenditures among major nations of the world; has avoided direct overseas military support; and acts as a status quo power par excellence. Yet, it is China that claims to be threatened by Japanese militarism and American and Japanese experts alike warn against rearmament by Japan, because it might provoke China to a belligerent posture!

The security problem China poses for Japan can be understood only in the broad framework of regional and global international affairs. This broader perspective permits issues such as Taiwan and rearmament to be seen in terms of the fundamental characteristics of the international system in which both nations participate, and it shifts emphasis away from conjecture about limitless specific scenarios that might lead to direct military confrontation between the two countries. During the 1960's, the global bipolar order gradually dissipated and the regional power balance underwent three upheavals, all directly touching on China. The Sino-Soviet split undercut the cold-war premise of the U.S.-Japanese Mutual Security Treaty and transformed regional power politics largely into a competition among the three great military powers. Chinese development of nuclear weapons in defiance of the superpowers added another dimension to East Asian politics. Finally, the war in Vietnam, which overshadowed East Asian international politics from 1965 to 1971, culminated in a radical reduction of U.S. forces and military commitments in the region and in the sudden initiatives to normalize Sino-American relations. This and the efforts by the United States government to cope with the serious trade and monetary problems growing out of the war led to severe strain in Japanese-American economic and political relations at the very moment when the regional power balance became very fluid.

Within the region, China presents the greatest security threat to Japan, in that both countries are engaged in Asia on several levels and place special priority on relations with nations in this area. The Japanese, although markedly more concerned about China's military power since a nuclear component was added, have downplayed the threat from Peking for obvious reasons. American commitments during the Vietnam War provided little room or incentive for gearing national security policy to issues beyond defense of the home islands. Moreover, the credibility of the United States was never seriously questioned until the dramatic economic and political moves by President Nixon in the summer of 1971. Most important, the Japanese have sought to avoid openly confronting China as a full-scale competitor because of the repercussions this would have throughout Asia and because a decision on rearmament would then be forced.

Few changes are likely to flow from diplomatic normalization that will basically affect the two nations' relations with each other. The very idea that Japanese diplomacy, with its record of equivocation and stolidity, will provide a unique bridge for communication or influence over the committed and strong-willed leaders of the greatest revolution in modern history beggars the imagination. Instead, China will have a better opportunity to fish in Japanese domestic politics and to try to wean Tokyo away from the United States. Moreover, beyond the short-term relaxation of tensions, it is difficult to identify ways in which the security relationship will be altered over the long run, even though some capacity to communicate is clearly better than none. Nevertheless, the key to international stability and peace in Asia extends far beyond bilateral political interchange and encompasses a complicated set of forces, fundamental to which is some sort of new regional military and political "power balance." It is gratuitous to assume that, following the reduction of the American military presence in East Asia, the Chinese will withdraw from all efforts to employ *Realpolitik* to expand their international influence because of "logistical weakness," the enormity of internal problems, or the like. China is still in the throes of revolution under a leadership militantly nationalistic, holding universalist and radical ideological commitments, and has close connections with sympathetic or allied revolutionary Communist groups in every underdeveloped Asian nation. Whatever the short-term effects of recognition might be, it seems possible, indeed likely, that the Chinese will ultimately stand as international competitors of the status quo-oriented Japanese, quite independently of the level of diplomatic intercourse that is established or the efforts of the Japanese to remain wholly aloof from all forms of power politics.

China's impact on Japanese security policy will grow out of a generally competitive international rivalry in East Asia and not from a direct bilateral military threat. The only direct military threat that China will pose to Japan over the next decade is nuclear and this would almost inevitably be linked to an external issue related to Japanese engagement in the region. However, for Japan to become a full-fledged competitor in international politics in East Asia would demand a security policy that involved conventional military capacities. Consequently, together with the status of the American alliance, relations with the People's Republic of China will be the critical influence on the timing and nature of Japanese rearmament.

Sino-Japanese trade has flourished, with one partner asserting the inseparability of politics and economics and the other rejecting this principle, and the actual pattern of bilateral relations graphically illustrates how difficult and complex it is to separate these two levels of international interaction. Despite the obviously political tone of Peking's policy, trade with Japan has rapidly developed essentially for economic reasons (indeed, out of necessity) in the shadow of bitter

anti-Japanese invective and Tokyo's continued close alliance
with the United States. Conversely, political considerations
have been integrally involved in Japan's "exclusively economic" policy. Virtually every move for increased trade has
involved, either directly or indirectly, a decision by the
Japanese government, including the extension of private credits as well as Import-Export Bank Loans. It is through the
sanctioning of expanded trade ties and the frequent and
varied "unofficial" missions to the mainland that de facto
political acceptance of Peking became a leading feature of
Japan's foreign policy in the 1960's. The two countries
generally complement each other economically in a manner
that leaves substantial latitude for future growth of trade, but
limits are imposed by the restricted appeal of Chinese exports
in Japan and by the long-term political uncertainties regarding the Communist regime. Because the Chinese are likely to
continue to pursue national economic self-sufficiency to an
extreme degree (the current ratio of imports to GNP approxi-
mates 3 percent, far lower than that of any other major
nation), considerable room will remain for them to manipu-
late trade for political ends even though the overwhelming
economic preeminence of Japan will restrict the effectiveness
of any maneuver of this sort. These factors leave the future
pattern of economic ties more conjectural than is normal in
bilateral relations of this sort. Politics and economics are in
this case integrally related, and the dimensions of Sino-
Japanese trade will ultimately depend on the broader competition between the two nations as major regional powers.

JAPAN, CHINA, AND AMERICA

Japan's future relations with China will be vitally affected
by a gradual weakening of the American alliance. The fundamental international forces sustaining the past close relation-

ship between the United States and Japan have been dramatically altered. Strategically, the military requirements for preserving America's more limited interest in Asia no longer demand an alliance with Tokyo.[9] Economically, Japan has moved from client relationship to that of economic competitor. Moreover, the American moves toward detente with China and Russia, together with a general relaxation of tensions in Asia have at least in the short run removed the possibility of an external threat to Japan. However, the ambiguity of the American position regarding future security commitments in Asia, partly a result of the fuzziness of long-term American goals and partly by calculation, has raised a question of credibility that with an external catalyst could serve as the stimulus for rearmament. No matter how uncertain American strategic commitments in Asia may be, the imperatives of global politics still require that the United States meet any threat from the Soviet Union. Consequently, the only power that could serve as that catalyst in the next decade is China.

What possible security threat can the Chinese pose for Japan? If the Japanese continue to limit their security zone solely to their home islands and to accept *in toto* the American nuclear guarantee, there is not likely to be a clear or present military danger to them from China, or from any other country, that could not be met by their own modest conventional defense forces. Yet, the Japanese government has acknowledged in various ways since 1965 that China does pose a security threat to Japan and that this threat has a nuclear dimension. As previously noted, a Chinese nuclear attack would certainly not be directed against Japan *in vacuo* but would involve Sino-Japanese conflict over an "outside issue" or over the conditions of alliance with the United States; that is, it would most likely take the form of nuclear blackmail. Thus, a China threat is tied to Japanese engagement in Asia, either through autonomous commitments integrally involving security considerations or through Japan's alliance with America. Japanese involvement in war through alliance with the United States is increasingly less probable, in view of continued strong resistance by the Japanese to direct involvement in American military moves and the increasing reluctance of America to make them. The option of total withdrawal from Asian security problems assured by the scope of past American actions cannot be held open much longer for the Japanese. Without isolation, a real or perceived threat from China could be indefinitely avoided only in the highly improbable event that international conflict is purged from Asia or that the Chinese effectively withdraw from regional politics. A Japan engaged in Asia can not be expected to depend entirely on American security policy in dealing with Peking, both because of the long-term unacceptability of such dependence to the Japanese and because the vicissitudes of international politics virtually preclude an absolute identity of interests for the two allies. The pressures for an independent military posture may then prove irresistible for Tokyo.

The suggestion of a rivalry between Tokyo and Peking extending to military matters seems at first glance somewhat inappropriate in the context of the current relaxation of tensions in East Asia. Yet even a cursory look beyond the recent headlines into the nature of foreign policymaking in Japan and the precarious balance of power in the region, raises doubts. Any effort to herald a new order in East Asia must be built on the ashes of the failures of the global superpowers to manage conflict in the region, and this alone will make all the more precarious efforts to establish stability without reliance on a military calculus. To hold that a low profile posture renouncing *Realpolitik* is a *possible* as well as desirable policy for Japan regarding China and East Asia[10] is to postulate a historically unprecedented pattern of international behavior, to assume the sudden eradication of the roots of conflict which have prevailed throughout the twentieth century in East Asia and to posit that the unique features of the U.S. alliance will persist under radically altered circumstances. In view of the inherent uncertainties of a multipolar world and the recent turbulent history of Asia, such assumptions are open to serious question. Intensified contacts between China and Japan add another complicating dimension to world politics, which provides little long-term assurance regarding peace in the area. What is certain is that the pattern of relations between Tokyo and Peking will be a recurring test of the Japanese-American alliance.

10

KIICHI SAEKI

Japan's Security in
a Multipolar World

THE U.S. RESPONSE TO A MULTIPOLAR WORLD

The world in the 1970's is said to be a multipolar world.
More accurately, it should probably be called a world of
political and economic multipolarity with military bipolarity.
A simplified characterization of the world in the 1970's as a
U.S.-Soviet-Chinese tripolar structure or a pentagonal structure with the addition of Japan and Western Europe could
very well lead to dangerous misunderstandings of reality.

It would appear that the American leadership now attaches
prime importance to adapting their policies to the new international environment which is increasingly multipolar in politics and economics alike. The so-called Nixon Doctrine is
designed to readjust the external role of the United States to
this changed context. It is quite natural to consider it unrealistic for the United States to continue playing the same
international role as in the past twenty-five years, since the
burdens of that role have exhausted her and led to a relative
decline in her national strength. Again, President Nixon's
desire to strike a bearable balance between American commitments abroad and national strength and the national interest is a very rational one.

Note: This article originally appeared in "East Asia and the World
System," *Adelphi Papers*, Number 92, published by the International
Institute for Strategic Studies, London, November 1972.

One cannot say, however, that the consequent readjust-
ment of American foreign policy has been entirely successful.
Confusion and contradictions can be perceived in it. Perhaps
this is partly due to the distortion of President Nixon's
purpose by tactics and rhetoric geared to the presidential
election campaign. More fundamentally, however, the cause
is probably to be found in the fact that the image of a future
multipolar world that he is aiming for, itself contains elements of ambiguity and confusion. At times he seems to
place the main emphasis on maintaining the bipolar military
structure and to use the concept of a multipolar political
structure as a cloak for stabilizing that structure, and as a
tactical aid in the United States' negotiations with the Soviet
Union. At other times he seems to stress the concept of a
pentagonal world as a rationale for alleviating the American
burden in relations with allies and for promoting the dialogue
and negotiations with countries hitherto hostile to the United
States. President Nixon has also stressed the necessity for
strength, partnership, and negotiations as means of adapting
to a multipolar world; and here he seems to be running the
risk of sacrificing partnership with long-standing allies for the
sake of furthering negotiations with long-standing enemies.
Sometimes, too, he seems to overemphasize the degree of
balance in the power relations in a five-polar political structure.

In a speech delivered at Kansas City in July 1971, President
Nixon stated that the United States was entering a period of
declining vitality, just as the Greeks and Rome had once
done, and predicted that within five to ten years, five great
powers—the United States, Western Europe, the Soviet
Union, China, and Japan—would control the world. Again, in
a special interview which appeared in *Time* magazine, he
expressed the opinion that if the United States, Europe, the
Soviet Union, China, and Japan could maintain a balance of

power among themselves, it would be a better and more stable world.[1]

If this opinion was a carefully considered one, what it means, as George Ball has pointed out, is a complete renunciation of the central strategy that the United States has followed since World War II.[2] It also suggests that the long-range strategy of the United States contains within it the possibility of Europe and Japan being treated eventually not as allies, but from the standpoint of American power politics on the same terms as the Soviet Union and China.

In Japan, the term "Nixon shock" refers to the announcement in July 1971 of President Nixon's plans to visit China; the announcement in August of a series of new economic policies including the imposition of a surcharge on American imports and the suspension of dollar convertibility to gold; and the subsequent textile negotiations ultimatum that went so far as to threaten Japan with the application of the Trading with the Enemy Act. This is supposed to have been a shock to Japan because there was no prior consultation with Premier Sato on the President's trip to China, or because the style of American diplomacy rubbed the Japanese the wrong way. It seems to me, however, that there is a more basic reason for the "Nixon shock." It was probably due to the fact that while the U.S. announcement of Presidential plans to visit China dramatically symbolized the end of the bipolar structure which had dominated the postwar world and the cold war, and the announcement of the New Economic Policy the collapse of the postwar international economic order known as the Bretton Woods system, neither announcement did much more than suggest considerable impending change and confusion in the future direction of American policy because of failure to set forth a clear vision or image of a new politico-economic order to replace the old.

THE JAPANESE RESPONSE TO A MULTIPOLAR WORLD

In these ambiguous circumstances, how should Japan cope with a world which is becoming multipolar? It is of fundamental importance that Japan should indicate her own vision as to how to cope with political multipolarity. One cannot be sure either that President Nixon's apparent vision of a multipolar political structure with a balance of power among the various poles is a carefully considered one or that the specific content of the Nixon doctrine is necessarily clear. In addition, both the Soviet Union and China seem to have their own respective images of the world which differ from that held by the United States. The fundamental aim of the Soviet Union will probably be to expand her external influence as much as possible while establishing a system of peaceful coexistence as well as the Soviet-American structure of military bipolarity. China seems neither willing nor able to rise to become a global power on a par with the United States and the Soviet Union. Her basic attitude is inward looking, and her efforts will be concentrated on consolidating her national strength and improving her domestic institutions for some years to come. Instead of challenging the Soviet Union or expanding her influence in competition with the United States and the Soviet Union, China seems intent upon establishing an international position shielded from the influence of the superpowers, while constituting herself as the protector of the Third World. Although European economic integration will probably make further advances, it is doubtful to what extent an economically integrated Europe will be able to push forward political integration and be able to exercise global influence. Also, one cannot be very optimistic about the extent to which the newly emerged countries of Asia will be able to gain strength and self-confidence and increase their regional solidarity, and the North-South problem will present as many difficulties as ever. In the final analysis, Japan will have to clarify her aims in coping with a multipolar world by studying the options open to her. The basic point here is the gap that is presently appearing, or that might possibly appear, between President Nixon's basic vision for coping with a multipolar world and the direction in which Japan is heading.

President Nixon appears to place Japan at one of the five poles of the balance of power, which should guarantee peace in a world marked by a relative decline in U.S. strength. He appears to think that it is unrealistic to expect a country, such as Japan, which is entirely dependent on another country for its security, to become a first-rate power and has said that there will clearly be a change in the U.S.-Japanese defense relationship as Japan regains her national strength and pride. He has warned that measures to maintain friendly relations will have to be adjusted to the changing world situation. He has also pointed out that the question is not so much whether Japan and the United States intend to maintain their mutually beneficial partnership, as how to inject into it the measure of reciprocity which is indispensable to its continuance.

In short, in President Nixon's image of the world, there seems to be an implicit expectation that Japan will be able to take up a position as one of the poles in the pentagonal political structure by becoming strong enough to maintain a partnership of equality and reciprocity with the United States. Naturally, the balance-of-power President Nixon is talking about does not mean simply a military balance of power. Nor is he saying that Japan might arm herself with nuclear weapons or that it is necessary for her to aim at becoming a military power in order not to be entirely dependent on another country for her security, and to introduce equality and reciprocity into her relationship with the United

States. Nevertheless, so long as President Nixon anticipates a pentagonal political structure with a balance among the five, and expects Japan to build herself up as one of the poles of such a balance, the logical conclusion is that the United States expects Japan to take the road towards becoming a military power.

If President Nixon's vision of a pentagonal political structure is indeed a carefully considered, deep-rooted one, and it gradually takes a clearer shape Japan, which up to now has maintained a close, cooperative relationship with the United States, will find herself forced to choose one of the following four courses: to build up military capacity to become a great power able to play a role as one of the five poles of the pentagonal world structure; to mobilize resources in other than military fields to produce the strength necessary to sustain a great-power diplomacy; to drop out of the role of a great power; or to try to adjust the discrepancies between Japan's own long-range vision and that of President Nixon.

THE FIRST ALTERNATIVE: NUCLEAR ARMAMENT AND MAJOR MILITARY POWER

Bearing in mind the nature of the world in the 1970's and the conditions governing Japan's role in it, an attempt to become a major military power continues to seem inappropriate: it would not only be undesirable for Japan, it could be dangerous.

Certainly, Japan should possess the defensive conventional armaments directly necessary to the protection of her own territory. Even here, there seems little need for their quantitative expansion beyond the present level, in the absence of any emergency or tension giving serious cause to fear a threat to Japan herself or the use of military pressure to force her to make political concessions.

In considering the size and nature of the self-defense forces which Japan should have for the 1970's, the three main aspects which would receive careful study are: securing safe trade routes for Japan; preventing conflicts over peninsulas and islands in close proximity to Japan and, in the event of such conflicts, not becoming entangled in them; and deterring strategic threats or pressure from the Continent against the political, economic, and military centers of Japan.

This first question basically lends itself to more effective solution through economic and diplomatic efforts, than through any military response. Any threat to marine transportation in peacetime should be identified as a challenge to the imperative rule of international law mandating freedom of navigation on the high seas and resolved diplomatically through international cooperation. Economic and diplomatic efforts are more effective means of alleviating animosity on the part of those who would threaten Japan's sealanes.

The question of how to safeguard maritime transport routes in case of a total war is a less important one than how to handle the third question. There is very little possibility of total war; and it is unlikely that any which should erupt would be protracted. Any limited war or conflict which might arise will be subject to considerable limitations of size, duration, and theater, and so stockpiling and alteration of trade routes are more effective means of coping with such an emergency.

In any event, protecting trade routes is no reason for expanding significantly the size of Japan's peacetime naval forces, although present strength levels are perhaps unsatisfactory.

With reference to the second question, one might reason that the possibility of international armed conflict involving Taiwan and the chances for Japanese or American involvement in such a conflict are virtually nil in view of the establishment of Sino-Japanese diplomatic relations on the heels of the Sino-American rapprochement. In the Korean Peninsula, efforts are being made in accordance with last July's joint communique by the Republic of Korea and the People's Democratic Republic of Korea toward relaxation of tension and the establishment of conditions for peaceful coexistence, paving the way for better mutual understanding and expanded exchanges between North and South, and leading to the peaceful unification of this divided country by the Korean people themselves. As long as the United States, China, the Soviet Union, and Japan, all of which have interests in the Korean Peninsula, are basically in a position from which they can support the Korean joint communique, one may assume that the trend is toward an easing of tensions in the peninsula. It would be difficult to argue that there is a greater need for stronger Japanese defense forces in order to prevent conflict in the Korean Peninsula from spilling over to Japan.

Although political instability may continue to plague Indochina even after the Vietnam War and the political situation in the Philippines, which is now under martial law, remains unstable, there is no need for Japan to increase her defense forces beyond their present level in order to prevent disputes from occurring in these areas, or to keep Japan from becoming involved in such conflicts. Such an approach would not be effective nor is it desired by the countries of Southeast Asia.

While the third question is by no means a pressing issue, it is one that no independent country can neglect. This question also relates to the issue of Japanese nuclear armament. However, it should be recognized that, basically, Japan can cope with the situation posed by this question only by relying upon the U.S.-Japanese Security Treaty.

It is of the utmost importance that Japan should draw a clear line between nuclear and nonnuclear armament. If Japan goes ahead with nuclear armament, it will become very difficult to control its level of military strength and set a clear limit to her armaments. So long as a policy of no nuclear armament is maintained, there is an automatic check on the scale of conventional armament as well. Large-scale use of conventional weaponry or of nonnuclear strategic offensive capacity would heighten the risk of nuclear intervention by either the enemy country or another power, and neither the use nor the maintenance of such conventional armaments would make sense to a country without the nuclear deterrent power to minimize the attendant risks.

In any case, Japan should not attempt to acquire nuclear weapons. First of all, Japanese nuclear armament is not as easy a matter as some foreigners may think. Any effort to revise the Japanese constitution in the ways necessary to legitimize the first steps to nuclear armament would stir up serious domestic social and political tensions. Technically, it would be almost impossible to find a place within Japanese territory to conduct nuclear tests. It would take at least ten years after making a political decision to reach the minimum meaningful level of nuclear armament, that is, one with some deterrent effect against a nuclear threat from China. And all this would be risked for the most doubtful gains. It is inconceivable that nuclear armament could more effectively guarantee Japan's security. The opposite is likely—that it would endanger both Japanese security and world peace. While Japan would have to pay a high price for nuclear armament, it would get no proportionate dividend in national security and would run great risks.

One reason for the scanty return from nuclear weapons is that Japan is small in area and densely populated: approximately 32 percent of Japan's total population is concentrated in the three separate 50-kilometer radial areas around Tokyo, Nagoya, and Osaka. This is also where important political, economic, and military functions are concentrated. Of all major countries, Japan is peculiarly vulnerable to nuclear attacks. Thus, if Japan wanted an effective nuclear deterrent against China, she would have to strive for sufficient superiority in nuclear armament to compensate for disadvantages in geographic and demographic conditions. At the very least, she would have to far surpass any rival so as to remove the fragility of her own nuclear defense. If Japan were to seek an advantage in nuclear armament over China, or concentrate greater efforts on nuclear armament than China, this might appear to Chinese eyes as Japanese military provocation. To foster China's hostility and an endless nuclear arms race with her would increase the threat to Japan rather than bolster her security.

Again, a decision by Japan to arm with nuclear weapons would perhaps invite a deterioration in relations with the United States, and it would most certainly not improve them. Since Japan's nuclear armament would be rooted in lack of confidence in the American nuclear deterrent, there is a danger that it would induce suspicion and resentment of Japan in the United States. As Japanese nuclear armament grew, this could, in some circumstances, drive U.S.-Japanese relations toward hostility. At the least, there is the risk that Japan's nuclear armament, far from supplementing the deterrent of the American nuclear umbrella, would replace it with a more fragile and less effective one.

If one adheres strictly to the logic that national security must be guaranteed by a national nuclear deterrent, to achieve a balance of power or offset a decline in the credibility of the American nuclear umbrella, Japan must be ready to deter any nuclear threat from the Soviet Union and United

States as well as from China. But there is no chance at all that Japan could, in the 1970's, develop the nuclear second-strike capability to maintain a balance of deterrence or military power with the Soviet Union and the United States, and scant possibility of this even in the 1980's. During all that time, Japan's efforts at nuclear armament would inject a dangerous degree of tension and confrontation into relations with both superpowers and constitute a challenge to the world peacekeeping mechanism, the core of which is the U.S.-Soviet bipolar military structure.

It should be recognized that the American nuclear umbrella under the U.S.-Japanese Security Treaty, although not without credibility problems, can provide better security for Japan than an independent Japanese nuclear arsenal. It is highly undesirable that Japan should strive for nuclear armaments to secure a balance of power. As President Nixon wrote in his "Building for Peace" report to the Congress: "Nuclear fighting power is the element of security our friends either cannot provide or could provide only with great and disruptive efforts. Hence, we bear special obligations towards non-nuclear countries."[3] Although one would like to think the United States will always be prepared to reaffirm this position, the fact that there seems to be some wavering on the part of American intellectuals on this point gives cause for concern. Zbigniew Brzezinski of Columbia University, for instance, has expressed the opinion that although nuclear proliferation was against the American national interest when the United States enjoyed nuclear superiority, it could be to her advantage in a situation of American-Soviet nuclear parity (and even more so should the United States be in a position of inferiority), since it could, in particular, complicate the strategic-political planning of the country in a position of nuclear superiority.[4]

THE SECOND ALTERNATIVE: EXPLOITATION OF OTHER
THAN MILITARY RESOURCES FOR GREAT POWER INFLUENCE

Granted, then, that there should be a curb on any great increase in Japan's military strength, it will be necessary to find effective ways to mobilize other factors of influence to sustain her vision and policy goals. The first priority in the 1970's will be to organize economic resources and activity as a means of diplomatic influence. The trend is toward ever stronger economic interdependence between nations, and many countries still seem to attach high priority to the pursuit of economic values. It should, therefore, be easy to transform economic capability and activity into political influence. In this field, Japan, the third-ranking economic power in the world, is blessed by the capacity to compete with any country, either as an equal or with the advantage.

Of course, Japan will not be able to make an adequate response to the multipolar world of the 1970's by economic diplomacy alone centering on aid and cooperation. Nevertheless, her highest priority will be not to build up military strength but to discover good ways to channel economic strength into political and diplomatic strength. Although one cannot claim that Japan has succeeded in this so far, there seems to be plenty of room for her to change her thinking and make an effort. From this point of view, Japan's economic assistance to Southeast Asia and economic cooperation in the development of Siberia are highly significant test cases. With foreign exchange holdings in excess of $17 billion and with long-term prospects for a continued favorable balance of payments amounting to more than 1 percent of GNP, Japan has sufficient accumulation of resources and power to enable her to venture a number of ambitious experiments in this area.

It will also be necessary for Japan to find ways of mobilizing diplomatic influence by means of culture, science, and technology. Basically, through comprehensive efforts in these spheres, she should muster all her energies to help create an international environment in which there is less dependence on military power.

THE THIRD ALTERNATIVE: RENUNCIATION OF A GREAT POWER ROLE

It remains doubtful that Japan will be able to become a great power and one of the poles of the pentagonal world envisaged by President Nixon either through a military build-up, or by exploiting her nonmilitary sources of power. Nevertheless, it would also be unrealistic for her to attempt to follow an existence unrelated to this multipolar political structure by deliberately renouncing any potential role as a great power. Japan cannot help but continue to have economic influence over other countries, as the third economic giant in the world, the second in the non-Communist world and the first of all the major economies in terms of growth, with the potential to become absolutely and relatively an even greater economic power than she is today. Given these facts, Japan cannot be irresponsible about her own influence. Nor can she be freed from the international role and responsibility of an economic power by dropping out as one of the poles of the multipolar political structure. Neutrality is only possible for countries which play a small role in shaping their environment; this is not, and cannot be, the case for a country of the size Japan has now become.

THE FOURTH ALTERNATIVE: READJUSTMENT OF U.S.-JAPANESE RELATIONS

What becomes necessary, then, is to adjust the contradictions between the Japanese vision and the American vision of a multipolar world. The nonmilitary future that most Japanese think desirable for Japan is possible only if there can be adjustment to the multipolar world envisaged by President Nixon. The precondition for Japan to walk the path of nonnuclear economic power is the continuation of the kind of relations between Japan and the United States, including the U.S.-Japanese Security Treaty, that would permit her to flourish. It is to be hoped that President Nixon's vision of a pentagonal political structure is flexible, or can be made flexible enough to embrace this kind of U.S.-Japanese relationship.

In a press interview in Tokyo on June 12, 1972, Henry Kissinger, then Special Assistant to President Nixon, indirectly suggested that the concept of a politically quintopolar system with balanced power relationships is not yet firm in President Nixon's mind. He stated that although the world is essentially bipolar in military terms it is economically multipolar, while politically it is somewhere in between. He also noted that the Security Treaty is necessary for the time being and that it should be maintained for the foreseeable future. He further indicated that he did not expect Japan to acquire nuclear arms.

One can no longer say, however, that the continuation of such a relationship is self-evident. This applies particularly to the Security Treaty. President Nixon, while affirming that the United States has no intention of entering into any agreements to promote communication with long-standing enemies which might sacrifice relations with long-standing allies, has not forgotten to warn of the need to adjust the means of expression of friendly relations as the world changes, and to anticipate changes in the U.S.-Japanese defense relationship as Japan regains her national strength and pride. There is a problem on the Japanese side as well. The political and social conditions for understanding and the acceptance by Japan of the equality and reciprocity wanted by the United States seem to have been weakened by increasing distrust of the United States, following the so-called "Nixon shock." There seems a growing possibility of considerable discrepancy between American and Japanese views as to what constitutes the equality and reciprocity to be introduced into the U.S.-Japanese partnership.

In any case, the adjustment of relations with allies and enemies in a world of political multipolarity is both complicated and fluid, and adjustment of U.S.-Japanese relations has become a problem too important and too complicated to be viewed with any complacency on either side. At the same time, the common interests of Japan and the United States in economics, security, and diplomacy, seem to be so broad and so entrenched as to warrant the assertion that there is no possibility at all that Japan might break with the United States, provided her choices are governed by reason. If, in spite of this fact, U.S.-Japanese relations seem fragile and feeble, this is because Japan is showing a tendency to want to keep her position of relative inferiority in the partnership with the United States, even in a future marked by a measure of instability, while the United States appears to be no longer willing to put up with such a relationship and is pressing Japan hard for equality and reciprocity.

A more basic problem which may be pointed out here is that, despite the strength of the United States and the weakness of Japan in their absolute sense, the relative decline in America's international influence and the relative increase in Japanese economic might has made it all the more difficult to introduce into their relationship those elements of equality and reciprocity which are essential for the maintenance of an effective partnership between the two countries. The problem is that the measures with which to judge equality and reciprocity in the relations between the two nations have grown confused, and the possibility of considerable discrepancy between American and Japanese conceptions of what is equal and what is reciprocal is increasing.

The U.S.-Japanese relationship cannot be defined in terms of a balanced, quintopolar political structure. The United States and Japan must perceive correctly the changes in the power relationship between them as well as the absolute gap between their magnitudes of power, and must strive for a common identification and understanding of the characteristics of equality and reciprocity which must be introduced into the relationship in order to maintain an effective U.S.-Japanese partnership. This means that equality and reciprocity in the overall U.S.-Japanese relationship must be sought. It would not be conducive to effective solution to perceive the relationship broken down into its separate economic, political, cultural, security, and other aspects, and then to seek equality and reciprocity in those fields in isolation.

One of the questions which is of increasing importance from the point of view of introducing equality and reciprocity in the relationship, yet which will likely defy easy solution, is that of the U.S. military bases in Japan. For the time being, however, the main priority is on solving economic problems. In a way, the fact that the relative economic strength of the United States has declined while Japan's economic might has shown a relative increase has confused the images of equality and reciprocity in the cooperative economic relations between the two nations, thus making it difficult to adjust these economic relations. This also means that, while the United States has come to feel that Japan's repayments in the economic arena are not commensurate with what she receives from the United States within the total context of the U.S.-Japanese relationship, including the security commitments, the Japanese public sees the situation as the exact opposite; all of which makes it necessary to adjust U.S.-Japanese economic relations in conjunction with security arrangements.

Economic issues will continue to be important to U.S.-Japanese relations in the future. The adjustment of U.S.-Japanese economic relations will be made all the more complicated if, the Vietnam War over and the United States relieved of her military burdens in Taiwan and Korea, the United States should succeed in a total revitalization of its economic power against the backdrop of rapprochement in its relations with the Soviet Union and China. The questions of economy and security are very closely related in U.S.-Japanese relations, and Japan will find it all the more necessary to promote greater cooperation in economic areas in order to promote greater cooperation in the defense field. However, it may be increasingly difficult in Japan for the Japanese government to obtain the support of all the people in such endeavors.

The U.S.-Japanese relationship must be developed in such a manner as to permit adaptation to the trend of political multipolarization. In this sense, it is desirable that issues between the two countries, whether they concern defense or economic matters, should be handled within a wider, multilateral framework rather than on a purely bilateral basis of Japan and the United States.

In economic terms Japan's relationship with the United States must be closer than with any other country. Yet to maintain this relationship effectively, Japan must be prepared to develop a cooperative tripolar relationship linking the United States, Europe, and Japan in such areas as currency, trade, investment, and economic assistance. Japan must also pay greater attention to developing varied relationships of cooperation with the emerging nations of East Asia and the rest of the world, China, and the Soviet Union, all of which are important to Japan as markets for Japanese products and

sources of raw materials. Particularly in her approaches to the
Soviet Union as a future supplier of energy resources Japan
must act with utmost prudence in consideration of adjustments in the U.S.-Japanese relationship of competition and
cooperation and Japanese relations with a China in conflict
with the Soviet Union.

It is desirable that security problems be handled in a wider
framework.

It would be better for U.S.-Japanese relations, in the fields
of security or economics, to be handled in a multilateral
framework rather than on a purely bilateral basis. To continue the Security Treaty is desirable, but it is neither desirable nor possible any more in a multipolar world for Japan to
depend decisively on the United States for any length of
time. To lessen Japan's dependence on the United States
while maintaining the Security Treaty it would be necessary
not to revise that treaty, but to try to fit it in with overlapping, multilateral security agreements.

Professor Shinkichi Eto of Tokyo University has proposed
the idea that the U.S.-Japanese security system be reinsured
by means of a Japanese nonaggression pact with China and
economic and cultural cooperation abroad. It may even become necessary to study the possibility and effectiveness of
reinsurance by means of a Soviet-Japan nonaggression pact,
despite the unpleasant memories such a pact would arouse.
Since the Soviet Union will probably be more bent on deterring the Chinese nuclear threat than the United States when a
stage of considerable advancement in Chinese nuclear armament has been achieved and she feels more directly threatened, one cannot deny the possibility that, from Japan's
point of view, the Soviet nuclear umbrella might more actively, and in another sense, deter the Chinese nuclear threat,
than would the American nuclear umbrella.

RELATIONS WITH CHINA AND THE SOVIET UNION

It is probably more realistic to understand a politically multipolar world in terms of a system more complicated and more fluid than a pentagonal architecture of mutually balancing powers. Just as the United States, as the curtain rises on an age of political multipolarity, is engaging in active negotiations and dialogue with both the Soviet Union and China, so Japan must discard the idea that she ought to stand against the Soviet Union and China so as to maintain relations of alliance with the United States. One might even say that the most effective way to maintain friendly relations with the United States is to improve relations with the Soviet Union and China. Perhaps a situation in which the United States lives in a state of peaceful coexistence, characterized by simultaneous negotiation and rivalry with both the Soviet Union and China, while tension between the Soviet Union and China continues short of war, may provide an international environment very much to the advantage of Japanese diplomacy, for such an environment could be expected to heighten the relative attractiveness of Japan to all three countries.

Although it is true that Japan's historical experience with the Soviet Union has bred distrust and caution, and her experience with China a strong interest mixed with familiarity and vigilance, Japan should in future attempt a rapprochement with both, keeping her distance from each as equal as possible, and not be bound by traditional concepts.

With the visit of Prime Minister Tanaka to China, the basic course for the normalization of Sino-Japanese relations was set. This may be characterized as the basic path to the normalization of diplomatic relations in such a way as would meet the test of time and lay the groundwork for long-term friendly relations between China and Japan. Specific steps to this end should, however, be implemented at a steady, unhurried pace. The basic path runs in the direction of "one China, not now" and recognition of the People's Republic of China as the sole, lawful government of China. It is a policy of maintaining existing economic relations with Taiwan as much as possible, despite the severance of formal diplomatic ties, and one in which neither Japan nor China seeks hegemony in Asia.

Japan's giant neighbor, the Soviet Union, has the potential to deal her a fatal blow and is the greatest rival of the United States, but is also, in view of her proximity, a promising future customer for Japanese industrial products and a major potential source of raw materials and energy. There are also several compelling reasons why the Soviet Union might want to improve relations with Japan, not the least being the rapprochement between the United States and China. Japan should work for rapprochement with the Soviet Union on the basis of sound calculations of interest and, without diluting her claim to her lost northern territories, Habomai, Shikotan, Etorofu, and Kunashiri, temper her inherited distrust from the past with an accurate objective appraisal of current possibilities.

Still, there is a limit to the unfolding of multilateral diplomacy to cope with an age of political multipolarity. There is probably no possibility, whatever, in the foreseeable future that Japan might get close enough to the Soviet Union and China to make Soviet-Japanese and Sino-Japanese relations equidistant with U.S.-Japanese relations, or profit by such a degree of rapprochement. It will take a long time to overcome completely the political, social, and institutional barriers which lie between Japan, the Soviet Union, and China respectively. In the foreseeable future, Japan's Security Treaty with the United States will continue to have greater significance than any possible security arrangements with other countries.

11

MORTON H. HALPERIN

U. S. - Japanese

Security Relations

The only remotely plausible change in the current alignment
of nations that would threaten the security of the United
States is for Japan to become hostile. Other conceivable
alterations are either extremely implausible—such as Western
Europe uniting in a way that created a threat of military
conflict between the United States and Western Europe—or
would not threaten American vital interests. The traditional
fears of American leaders that Japan or Western Europe
would come under the domination of Russia, China, or a
Communist bloc now appear unfounded. Nor is it likely that
a single power would come to dominate the Asian area.

Not the least important of the gains resulting from the
U.S.-Japanese alliance is that neither country has had to take
account of the possibility of hostility between them. However, the relation has always been an uneasy one and much of
the cement holding it together until now has been weakened
by events of the past few years. A deterioration—even a rapid
and substantial one—cannot be ruled out over the decade
unless both countries move to put the relationship on a new
footing reflecting both their common interests and potential
conflicts.

Note: Parts of this chapter were published originally by the Jiji Press
in an article by Morton H. Halperin, "U.S.-Japanese Relations: The
Changing Context," *Pacific Community* (October 1973).

THE DIVERGENCE OF EXPECTATIONS

Since the beginning of the effort to forge a new postwar relationship between the United States and Japan, leaders of the two countries have looked at the same thing and seen something totally different. The divergence in perception has in turn led to different explanations of events and different expectations of the relationship.

The Mutual Security Treaty between the United States and Japan has itself been seen in very different ways by leaders in the United States and in Japan. For many Americans the treaty is unequal in that it obligates the United States to defend the security of Japan without requiring the Japanese government to assume a mutual obligation toward the United States. Indeed, these are the literal terms of the treaty and, in American eyes, Japan is the major beneficiary. The United States takes on an added security burden, while Japan gets a "free ride."

Americans critical of Japan habitually apply the "free ride" label to the Mutual Security Treaty, citing it as a major factor in Japan's economic success. The United States, they point out, has consistently spent 7-10 percent of its GNP on defense, while Japan has consistently spent less than 1 percent. The amount that Japan has saved on defense, it is argued, has been applied to industrial development, which has flooded the American market with highly competitive Japanese products. Thus, according to this view, Japan has serious obligations to the United States because of the benefits accrued from the Mutual Security Treaty. By virtue of this "free ride," therefore, Japan should be willing to cooperate with the United States: to provide the bases and the political support necessary to the United States for its security obligations in the Far East; and to use its economic power consistent with American objectives, particularly in support of the American dollar.

Many Japanese observers also label the Mutual Security Treaty unequal, for quite different reasons. Most American officials occupying high positions in the American government today have no direct memory of the early postwar period; they do not know how the Mutual Security Treaty came into existence or what the positions of the two countries were at the time. These events were much less important to the history of the United States than to the history of Japan. Most Japanese officials now in high positions remember that period vividly, because they were then active in Japanese-American relations either as junior bureaucrats or junior members of the Diet. For these Japanese, the Mutual Security Treaty was an obligation imposed on Japan as one of the prices Japan had to pay for gaining independence in the form of a peace treaty which was, in Japanese eyes, remarkably mild. Japanese remember that the United States insisted the Mutual Security Treaty be contracted at the same time as the Peace Treaty and they have little doubt that the United States would not have agreed to end its occupation of Japan if Japan had not been willing simultaneously to sign a Mutual Security Treaty. Thus the treaty is, for many Japanese, something imposed on Japan during the occupation period and not something freely chosen by the Japanese people after they regained their sovereignty. They feel that such an unequal treaty must ultimately be abrogated and replaced by some other arrangement perhaps even a similar treaty entered into freely by a sovereign Japan.

Closely related to the differing expectations about the Mutual Security Treaty are the divergent views of the American military presence in Japan and the number of American bases on Japanese territory. Many Americans look upon the base problem through a lens conditioned by their experience with the Federal Republic of Germany. The Federal Republic views American bases in Europe as vital to its security. Opposing military forces directly confront each other on the European continent. The German government, having faced invasion from the Soviet Union in the past, has been particularly concerned about a confrontation and is anxious to keep as many American troops as possible in the Federal Republic. Thus, in dealing with Germany, the United States confronts an ally eager to have American troops and willing to do what it can to maintain American bases. It is this perception of the value of bases to an ally that has been carried over by many American officials into their evaluation of the Japanese situation. The assumption has been that the Japanese government's attitude is the same as that of the Federal Republic. In short, many Americans believe that Japan is anxious to have as many U.S. troops as possible in Japan and therefore would be willing to pay a price to maintain those forces. The American bases, as the treaty itself, have been seen as something the United States is doing for Japan. The bases and, hence, the credibility they lend to the American deterrent for Japan have been a favor by the United States that requires Japanese reciprocation.

For many Japanese the situation is completely opposite. American bases in Japan are seen as an extension of the occupation of Japan by the United States. Many Japanese do not see any immediate and direct conventional threat to Japan because it is separated by large areas of water from its potential opponents in the Soviet Union and perhaps China. Most Japanese have not considered the bases necessary to the credibility of the American nuclear guarantee. Even those who have desired some American military presence in Japan have felt that there are too many American bases, occupying very valuable Japanese real estate, and have been advocating a substantial reduction in the American presence.

Most Japanese see the bases as part of the American security commitment to other countries in the area, including Korea, Taiwan, and Thailand. Thus Japan is doing the United States a service by providing real estate on the crowded Japanese islands for bases that the American military see as essential for meeting American commitments to other nations. These commitments were not made in consultation with Japan and are not commitments that Japan enjoys sharing with the United States. Thus for many Japanese, the bases represent, at best, a *quid pro quo* for the American deterrent. The United States agrees to provide a nuclear guarantee to Japan, and in return Japan makes available bases which the United States uses to meet its security commitments to other nations.

These mutual misperceptions about the nature of the security treaty and of U.S. bases in Japan were reflected also in the assessments by Americans and Japanese of the American decision in 1969 to agree to the reversion of Okinawa to Japan.

For most Americans, the willingness of the President to agree to the reversion of Okinawa in 1969 represented a magnanimous act involving potential cost to the American government with no benefit. In particular, they pointed to the fact that it occurred while the Vietnam War was still in progress and American bases on Okinawa were heavily engaged in that effort. There were no interest groups in the United States pressing for reversion and none had anything to gain from it. On the contrary, the American military and American businesses with interests on the island were known to be in favor of maintaining American control over Okinawa. Nevertheless, according to this view, the United States went forward with reversion because Japanese leaders stated that it was essential to Japanese domestic politics. To Americans, this gesture of magnanimity required a political favor in return from Japanese Prime Minister Sato. The Nixon administration expected the Japanese government at least to show similar sensitivity to its domestic political needs.

This perspective on Okinawa reversion led, in particular, to the American belief that Prime Minister Sato should be willing to make a concession by restricting Japan's export of synthetic textiles to the United States, an issue that had domestic political value to President Nixon. The President, while campaigning for office, had promised his supporters that he would secure an agreement limiting textiles. To fulfill this obligation the President and his associates sought Japanese cooperation and warned, moreover, that failure to reach an agreement on textiles would further complicate U.S.-Japanese economic relations and might even prevent Senate ratification of the Okinawa reversion treaty. Given the American perception of the Okinawa issue, it was quite natural to expect reciprocation on textiles and quite natural to feel that the two issues should be linked.

The Japanese perception of Okinawa, however, made any explicit linkage of the issues impossible. From the Japanese perspective, by refusing to return the administrative rights over Okinawa to Japan, the United States was continuing to occupy and rule Japanese territory twenty-five years after the war and long after the United States and Japan had become close allies. For the entire postwar period the U.S. government had maintained that it intended to control these islands as far ahead into the future as one could foresee. It was only when left-wing pressure in Japan made it imperative that something be done that American officials began seriously to consider reversion. For most Japanese, reversion was by this time long overdue. Japan had demonstrated that it was a good and loyal ally and had, among other things, permitted bases in Japan itself to be used by the United States. It was unreasonable for the United States to expect to occupy indefinitely a substantial portion of Japanese territory. Thus reversion, agreed to in 1969, came just in time to avoid a serious disruption of U.S.-Japanese relations. While showing some gratitude for those in the American government who worked for reversion, the general Japanese attitude was that reversion was long overdue and that Japan had already paid for it.

DIVERGENT AMERICAN IMAGES

Thus far I have discussed American images of Japan as if there was a single American view. In fact, however, different Americans in policy-making roles have very different views of Japan and of the nature of U.S.-Japanese relations. In general, there seem to have been three basic approaches to Japan among U.S. policy makers in the postwar, or more accurately, the post-Korea period. While it is possible to identify three distinct phases in postwar U.S.-Japanese relations, according to which of these views was dominant, all three views have been present to some degree at all points in the postwar relationship.

The first of these views can be identified as "inevitable harmony." Roughly, that is the notion that the interests of the United States and Japan are identical and that Japan can be counted upon to act as an agent of the United States in Asia. The second view comprises the idea of "creating a partnership" through diligent efforts on both sides to overcome the differences inherent in the two cultures, as well as divergent national interests. Finally, the third view, which includes a multitude of pessimistic feelings about the future of the relationship, is one of an "inevitable conflict of inter-

ests" between the United States and Japan. This last view is a
less coherent philosophy about the relationship and serves
more as a catchall category for a variety of tactical and ad
hoc approaches to the relationship. To characterize the postwar period in terms of these three views, it could be said that
U.S.-Japanese policy has been motivated primarily by a combination of the first two images, with elements of distrust
(the third image) lurking in the background and occasionally
coming to the fore when domestic politics enter into the
relationship.

To an extent, these three divergent views are characteristic
of different interests within the policy-making elite The
dominance of any one of these views at a particular point in
time can be related to the influence that a particular part of
the bureaucracy has over the policy-making process. Therefore, in describing these three views, an attempt will be made,
as far as possible, to relate them to particular sections of the
bureaucracy and to describe their role in policy making at
various points in the postwar relationship.

Inevitable harmony. The idea of inevitable harmony seems
to have characterized the period in U.S.-Japanese relations
extending from the occupation to the early 1960s, when
Edwin Reischauer became ambassador. During this period
American policy toward Japan was dominated by a sense that
Japan's future was inseparably linked to that of the United
States. The United States had been instrumental in fashioning
the postwar political and economic structure of Japan and
Japan had accepted dependence on the United States for
both economic and security assistance. It was inevitable that
the national interests of both countries would be parallel,
especially since the United States had done so much for
Japan and Japan had so much reason to be grateful.

The idea of inevitable harmony is in many ways a grand
scheme for the protection of U.S. security interests in Asia. It

envisions an economically strong, rearmed Japan promoting the interests of the United States in Asia and relieving the United States of a substantial portion of its burden.

Those who have advocated Japanese rearmament have generally based their case on arguments suggesting inevitable harmony. A rearmed Japan would inevitably pursue a course consistent with that of the United States. To civilian policy makers this would permit the United States to decrease its defense expenditures. To military leaders it would complement and strengthen U.S. efforts.

Creating a partnership. Perhaps more than any other single event, the public dissent in Japan over the revision of the Security Treaty caused American decision makers to begin reassessing the relationship. In the process of reevaluation, the voice of those advocating the development of a partnership began to dominate. Just after the events of 1960, Edwin O. Reischauer wrote an article in *Foreign Affairs* about the "broken dialogue" between the United States and Japan, pleading the case for the United States to begin looking at Japan more carefully and to consider that Japan was going to have its own set of national interests. Shortly after this article, he was appointed U.S. ambassador to Japan by President Kennedy. His appointment was seen as a recognition by the President of the growing importance of Japan and the need to establish a dialogue with the Japanese that would compensate for the many differences between the two cultures. In 1964, affirming the wisdom of Reischauer's appointment, George Kennan wrote, "The tasks of intellectual mediation between these two countries, where the technical difficulties of communication are truly formidable, is one for specialists. It is not accomplished as many Americans like to believe, merely by thrusting ordinary people together and 'letting them get to know each other.' "[1]

Thus during the period of the 1960's, the attitude of U.S.

policy makers toward Japan came to be characterized more by the "partnership" image than by either of the other two images. However, it is also evident that this was a period in the U.S.-Japanese relationship when policy was left pretty much in the hands of the experts. Neither the memoirs of the Kennedy years nor Johnson's *Vantage Point* give more than passing reference to Japan; Japan was not on the front burner in the White House. U.S. policy toward Japan was influenced very much during this period by the middle-level bureaucrats in both the State Department and Defense Department, most particularly those who had a continuing interest in U.S.-Japanese relations.

Basically, the "partnership" image is predicated on the assumption that there are strong mutual interests between the two countries and that usually the leaders of the two countries share a common outlook. But it also recognizes the difficulties of overcoming cultural and other differences between the two countries to create a workable relationship. At the same time, tactical differences and domestic pressures are strong enough to sour the relationship, if measures are not taken to ease their effect. In other words, the relationship is bound to be strong and friendly in the long term, if the inevitable short-term difficulties are handled with care.

The "partnership" image envisions an economically and politically strong Japan, participating independently in world affairs. While recognizing the importance of the security relationship, advocates of partnership are especially concerned about any manifestations in U.S. policy toward Japan that would indicate a U.S. desire to see Japan rearm or that would encourage any militaristic feeling in Japan.

In its most refined form the "partnership" image advises that both American and Japanese leaders be more aware of the influence of domestic politics on the relationship and begin to compensate in their dealings with each other, with the hope of avoiding placing themselves in intractable positions by responding too blindly to these domestic pressures. A sense of history and continuity is advocated for all official actions that are taken relevant to Japan. However, it is recognized, with frustration, that the public media on both sides tend to skew the significance of points of contrary interest in the U.S.-Japanese relationship.

It can probably be said with confidence that this "partnership" image, the voice of reason and understanding, has really been the most important in shaping postwar relations between the United States and Japan, in spite of manifestations of the other two images in U.S. policy from time to time. The "partnership" image is certainly the attitude reflected through the years in annual presidential messages on relations with Japan. Even according to the most recent Nixon statements, for example, U.S. government policy is described as the promotion of a cooperative political interdependence, based on increasing economic interdependence within the context of the worldwide competitive system.

Inevitable conflict of interests. There is probably no point in the postwar U.S.-Japanese relationship where it would not be possible to find some trace of lingering animosity and distrust toward Japan among American policy makers. In 1949, during the period when most were feeling very magnanimous toward Japan, the Secretary of the Army, Kenneth Royall, caused a small storm when he was reported to have said: "We don't owe the Japanese anything, not even a moral obligation. We had the right—and the duty—to disarm them after the war, even though someone else may later cut their throats."[2] And a decade later Hanson Baldwin was editorializing that "the military chauvinism—never far beneath the surface in the Japanese—is still there, encouraged perhaps by a subconscious desire to get back at the conquerors."[3]

Many feel now that the image, or the style, being projected

by the White House in its dealings with Japan betrays a sense of inevitable conflict, if not economic, then political. Observers are further disturbed by the fact that this approach is the style of a minority, and the majority's plea for temperance is going unheeded. The fear is that Japan will become so alienated by this rough treatment that she will take off down a road toward goals quite incompatible with U.S. interests. As William Bundy describes it: "What Americans must face up to is that their government's behavior toward Japan in the last year has created resentment and suspicion that will linger for a long while . . . A Japan alienated from the United States is not likely to rush into the arms of Peking. Paradoxically, but about as surely as one can predict anything, the effect of such alienation would be to make Sino-Japanese rivalry naked and sharp. Then, unhappily, the U.S. would be back in the situation Professor Iriye has described, forced to choose sides between China and Japan—and headed for inevitable conflict."[4]

The White House seems to believe that the Japanese must be shocked into action. U.S. actions seem calculated to break Japan's psychological dependence on the United States and to make Japan realize that, now that she has reached great-power status, she can no longer expect favored treatment from the United States. The total effect of this style of relations is to imply that there is no permanent alliance between the United States and Japan and that Japan should stand on its own feet in a free-wheeling world dominated by several interacting powers.

There are those critics who feel that the White House is going through a period of power politics, where the main actors on the international scene can only be the nuclear powers. Thus, despite lip service to the objective of a five-power world, Japan does not really fit in if it is only an economic power. Both this policy objective and certain statements by Pentagon officials have caused the Nixon administration to present the image that it expects Japan to become a nuclear power—that the acquisition of nuclear weapons by Japan is inevitable.

Despite a very vocal opposition the White House has a number of constituencies from which it draws support and encouragement in its rough handling of Japan. First, there is a group of American leaders from all sections of the government who feel burdened by the relationship with Japan. They sense that Japan has been expecting too many concessions from the United States and that Japan relies too heavily on U.S. support in its dealings with other countries. What this group ascribes to is really a version of the "free ride" argument, because behind their frustration is a belief that Japan is taking the United States for a ride politically by refusing to take its own political initiatives internationally.

The second and most readily identifiable constituency for the "inevitable conflict" image comprises U.S. business leaders and their government representatives. American business in general has been frustrated by the unique ability of the Japanese to manage the few advantages they have in the world market. American companies have felt that trade relations are unfair because of the severe restrictions in Japan on U.S. investment and imports. Some business leaders have developed the idea that Japan has been working overtime at the expense of its population, to penetrate the American market. There have been further indications of the idea, among both industry and government leaders, that there is some mysterious relationship between Japanese industry and government that makes it possible to mobilize resources for a very precise economic assault on the world. Some sections of the Commerce and the Treasury Departments, for example, are convinced that Ministry of International Trade and Industry (MITI) should be examined and emulated in order to discover the key to this phenomenon, when in fact MITI may have been more of a hindrance than a help in the Japanese export drive.

There are really two subgroups among those ascribing to the "inevitable conflict" image of Japan. The first group believes that there is really nothing we can do to prevent or even forestall conflict with Japan—that Japan will only act in its own self-interest. Whatever measures we might devise to satisfy Japan would necessarily be contrary to our national interest. The other group, while agreeing that the long term will bring conflict, feels that short-term measures can at least forestall friction. Taking the "partnership" image in reverse, they see short-term partnership and long-term conflict. They would say that only the political arrangements the United States has made for Japan since World War II have kept Japan in line. The idea is that all the ingredients for a pre-World War II Japan are there; we must do what we can to mute their development.

During the 1970's, the image of inevitable conflict has dominated American policy toward Japan, undoubtedly a consequence of the extreme concentration of policy making in the hands of a single architect. One man can't possibly respond appropriately to all people, and one of the victims of this situation has been Japan. Although some concessions have been made to the relationship with Japan, on balance Henry Kissinger appears to believe that Japan will inevitably assume a posture distinct from, if not hostile to, the United States. At least since 1971, the clear message of the Nixon administration has been that the close postwar relationship between the United States and Japan is no longer appropriate in a five-power world where each power must balance its relations with the other four.

The Japanese, like everyone else, look primarily to the President and Henry Kissinger for the formulation and articulation of U.S. policy toward Japan. The record of White House statements and actions since 1971 has not reinforced Japanese confidence in the strength of the U.S.-Japan partnership. On the contrary, it has tended to enhance the appeal of those in Japan who warn that close alliance with the United States is not destined to serve Japan's best interests. Thus the psychological base for a competitive relationship between the United States and Japan has already been nurtured.

THE CONSEQUENCES OF COMPETITION

Should the two countries begin to drift apart, their conflicting interests could cause an acceleration of the process of deterioration. A trade war, for example, could lead Japan to seek ways to expand trade with China and the Soviet Union, leading to closer political relations with these countries. This in turn could cause disquiet in the United States. Similarly, competition between the United States and Japan for markets in the developing states of Asia and Latin America could lead to political competition. As the gulf widened, Japanese leaders might conclude that they could no longer rely on American security guarantees and that Japan needed a vastly increased defense effort, including the procurement of nuclear weapons. To secure a consensus for rearmament Japanese leaders would have to appeal to nationalistic and at least latently anti-American sentiments in Japan. Japanese rearmament in such a setting would not only be a substantial setback to American nonproliferation efforts but would arouse intense concerns throughout Southeast Asia, decreasing the prospects for stable development.

Deterioration in U.S.-Japanese relations need not go this far, even if the intimacy of the past cannot be maintained. However, given the potential for disagreement, once the feeling of closeness is lost, the drift will almost certainly be substantial. In fact, one cannot rule out the possibility that the change will be even more fundamental. Between major powers with the economic potential to damage each other seriously, intermediate positions between alliance and hostility tend to be unstable.

If the bounds of alliance were broken and disputes between Japan and the United States began to occupy the attention of both governments, military planners on both sides would begin to notice that some of the pressures which made for conflict in the past still exist. For example, the growing Japanese influence in the greater East Asian area, which many Americans now see as desirable, could be seen as a threat if Japan were considered potentially hostile.

Territorial disputes between the two countries are also not inconceivable. Japanese economic interests in the Trust Territories of the Pacific are growing and many Japanese still remember their period of control over this area. Although most Japanese do not consider these territories to be inherently Japanese—as they do Okinawa, the Bonins, and the northern territories held by the Soviet Union—if Washington does not find a way to bring the territories into a permanent association with the United States in a manner acceptable to the residents of the islands, and if U.S.-Japanese relations turn sour, the Trust Territories peoples might well turn to Japan for support. A Japanese government that viewed the United States as increasingly hostile might be tempted to intervene, and the Trust Territories could loom as a potential territorial conflict of significant proportions.

If each came to think about the other as a potential enemy there would be substantial cost to both of them. Japan, confronted with the possibility of needing to treat the United States as a potential enemy, would not only have to rearm very substantially and build a nuclear capability but would also have to alter its relations with the Soviet Union and China in order to avoid a two-front conflict situation. The domestic impact of such a change in Japanese posture would be difficult to calculate. On the American side, some increase in defense expenditures would almost certainly be necessary. The United States would also become concerned with the extent to which some of its advanced industries were dependent on production in Japan. Trade restraints would be expanded to the detriment of both nations.

One does not have to believe that there is any substantial possibility of relations deteriorating this far to accept the great value to both countries of continuing a close relation. The cost of any drift apart would be significant enough to justify concern, even if the probability of a rift occurring seems very small.

THE FUTURE OF U.S.-JAPANESE RELATIONS

The future of U.S.-Japanese relations will depend in part on the evolution of domestic politics within the two countries. In the United States the critical uncertainty will be whether the next administration, which comes to power in 1977, will continue to concentrate all responsibility in the hands of a few officials. In the interim, policy toward Japan will also be affected by the strength of the presidency and the relative roles to be played by Congress and by career officials in major departments, including the State Department. On the Japanese side, the critical variable is the future role of the Liberal Democrats.

Leaving aside the uncertainties of domestic politics, which will be influenced primarily by concerns other than U.S.-Japanese relations, what can be said about the future of the relationship? In particular, what can be done by individuals and groups in both countries who believe that a close and

strong U.S.-Japanese relationship is vital to the security of
the two countries and to the evolution of East Asia?

It is perhaps worth remarking on the strength the relationship has shown in the period of trial experienced over the last
few years. Despite the difficulties, solutions have been found
for pressing bilateral problems and the two countries have
maintained a constructive dialogue with each other. Perhaps
of more significance, the period has seen the solution of most
of the outstanding bilateral problems between the two countries. The Okinawa treaty has been ratified by the U.S.
Senate and the Japanese Diet, and Okinawa has been returned
to Japan, ending the last legacy of the occupation. The
textile issue has caused considerable difficulty and confusion,
but nevertheless it also has been settled. There are no current
outstanding demands from a particular American industry
and this set of bilateral issues may not arise again.

Economic relations between the United States and Japan
are likely to be perceived more and more as part of multilateral problems involving the developed countries of Western
Europe and, in some cases, the world economy as a whole.
The period in which bilateral economic issues have come to
dominate U.S.-Japanese relations may, in retrospect, be seen
as a relatively brief interlude during the early 1970s. By the
end of the decade the security and diplomatic issues are
likely to dominate U.S.-Japanese relations again. In that
context it will be important to confront all the different
perceptions of the U.S.-Japanese relationship discussed
above. The two countries will need to develop a common
perception of security problems in Asia, a common concep-
tion of the role of the Mutual Security Treaty and of American military presence in Japan. Neither country now appears
ready for a sustained dialogue on these questions at the
official level.

In the United States, a major policy making is so concentrated in the White House and in the personal office of the Secretary of State that officials in both the State and Defense Departments are simply not in positions to engage in authoritative discussions on basic security problems. The efforts to develop a common China policy in the early months of the Nixon administration demonstrate the futility and danger of attempting to develop common policies when the officials on one or both sides simply lack the authority to do so. Japanese and American officials thought that they had developed an agreed approach to the China problem, only to learn that the Nixon White House was off on its own arranging a Presidential trip to Peking.

In the interim, therefore, the most useful thing will be for officials in both governments and scholars concerned about U.S.-Japanese relations to begin to try to think through the problems of developing a common approach to security problems in the new era of detente. Such discussions will be useful when both governments are in a position to begin serious negotiations. Japanese need to determine the degree to which Japan wishes to have an independent policy and the degree to which its security does depend on the maintenance of the American alliance system and the presence of some American forces in Japan. American officials need to determine the nature of American security interests not only in Japan but in other countries in East Asia in the light of the new relationship with China and the developing detente with the Soviet Union. Before too long, officials of the two governments will need to come together to try to develop a common approach to these problems which can be the basis for either the revitalization of the existing Mutual Security Treaty or a negotiation of a new treaty based on the perceived common interest of the two nations.

It is also important to develop a wider range of contacts between Japanese and Americans. In this connection, the

establishment of the Japan Foundation and the encouragement of Japanese studies in the United States with growing
support from Japanese business are of great significance. Of
equal importance would be the increase in American studies
in Japan. While the growth of Japanese tourism means that
many more Japanese will have at least a superficial exposure
to American culture, it is vital for Japanese to get better
training in their universities on the nature of American politics and the American political system.

It is almost certain that the early 1970's will be looked
upon in retrospect as a transition period in U.S.-Japanese
relations. The United States during this period has put aside
its efforts to isolate China and has sought in its dealings with
the Soviet Union to reduce the danger of nuclear war. During
this period also, the United States has been preoccupied with
withdrawing from Vietnam and attempting to develop a new
consensus for American involvement in the world in the
post-Vietnam period.

Japan is seeking to come to grips with its new status as a
major actor on the international economic scene. Japanese
leaders are also seeking to define a new Japanese political role
in the world in the light of the end of the postwar period.

It is perhaps not surprising at such a time that U.S.-Japa-
nese relations should appear to run into some difficulties.
Perhaps some assurance can be taken from the fact that,
despite the constraints, leaders on both sides of the Pacific
continue to voice the need for a close relationship. As long as
influential voices in both countries are being raised in support
of a close U.S.-Japanese relationship, the real common interest of the two sides is such that the transition period is likely
to come to an end with Japan and the United States closer
together and committed to the pursuit of common interests.

Notes

Notes to Chapter 2

1. Isaiah Ben-Dasan, *The Japanese and the Jews*, (New York: John Weatherhill, 1972).
2. This percentage is increased somewhat when the "conservative" candidates who ran as "independents" and joined the LDP after election are taken into consideration. The unaffiliated candidates accounted for 6.2 percent of the votes in the 1972 election, about 3-4 percent of which went to the "independent" conservatives.
3. Ishida Hakuei made this forecast in 1961 in the *Chuo koron* (April 1963).
4. Junnosuke Masumi, "Seiji katei no henbo" (The changing political process), in Yoshitake Oka, ed., *Gendai nihon no seiji katei* (The political process in modern Japan; Tokyo: Iawanami Shoten, 1958), pp. 317-386.
5. One exception, it should be noted, is the Democratic Socialist party which has stood for less military cooperation with the United States but has emphasized the importance of cooperation in general.
6. Etatism implies dependence on and expectations of the state. Theoretically the Socialists and Communists stand for more state intervention in the management of society, as has usually been the case in other countries. In Japan, however, they have taken the opposite position. For example, they were opposed to the recentralization of the police in the beginning of the 1950's and have argued for a larger power in local government. Whether it is merely a tactical position or genuine departure from the orthodox position is yet to be seen.
7. The two exceptions were the elections of 1922 and 1947. In the first case, the cabinet in power at the time of the election was merely an interim cabinet. In the latter, Japan was under occupation and the government party was not really in power. Moreover, SCAP, at that

time, rather favored the JSP over the conservatives, who had been in power and were defeated.

8. Herman Kahn, *The Emerging Japanese Superstate* (Englewood Cliffs, N.J.: Prentice Hall, 1970), chap. 2.

9. Junichi Kyogoku, *Gendai minshusei to seijigaku* (The modern democratic system and political science; Tokyo: Iwanami Shoten, 1969), pp. 148-153.

10. Zbigniew Brzezinski, *The Fragile Blossom* (New York: Harper and Row, 1972).

11. The best example, though historical, is the confusion that resulted from the ratification of the London Naval Treaty of 1930. The government and the Naval Command could only arrive at a compromise in vague terms, which as students of Japanese history well know caused a great deal of confusion later.

12. Another important factor preventing the Japanese from acting with foresight is their view of world affairs, in which the world situation is considered to be a "given" to which Japan must adapt and not something to which the Japanese can make a contribution. Several scholars have pointed out this defect. For example, Tetsuro Watsuji noticed it before the war and Junichi Kyogoku after the war. Junichi Kyogoku, p. 170.

13. As Gunnar Myrdal pointed out more than a decade ago, unfortunately tension exists between the management of international economy and the welfare state that pursues such objectives as income assurance and full employment. Developments within the United States and Europe have tended to vindicate his observation.

14. The basic instrument has been subsidy policy and protection.

15. Votes and seats of each party.

Year	LDP	JSP	DSP	Komeito	JCP
1958	57.8 (percent)	32.9	–	–	2.6
	287 (seats)	166			1
1960	57.5	27.5	8.8	–	3.0
	296	145	17		3
1963	54.7	29.0	7.4	–	4.0
	283	144	23		5
1967	48.8	27.9	6.2	5.4	4.8
	277	140	30	25	5
1969	47.6	21.4	7.7	10.9	6.8
	288	90	30	47	14

Year	LDP	JSP	DSP	Komeito	JCP
1972	46.8	21.9	7.0	8.5	10.5
	271	118	19	29	38

Source: Kokkai binran (Diet directory; Tokyo: Nihon Keizai Shimbun, 1974).

16. The successes of the JCP also makes forecasting more difficult. Before the gains of the 1972 election, there was talk about a coalition among the DSP, Komeito, and the JSP. Now a coalition between JCP and JSP is as likely as the former.

17. Remarks made by Toshio Tamaguchi in *Jiyu* (May 1971).

18. Percentage of popular support for the five parties before 1972.

Party	Total
LDP	40
JSP	18
Komeito	4
DSP	3
JCP	3
Others	1
No party	29
No answer	2

Source: *Mainichi shimbun*, November 24, 1972.

19. The bulk of social investment in Japan must come from the government budget, the money for which is raised through taxes or government bonds. Increased taxation is difficult for a government that does not have massive support; conservatism in financial and bureaucratic circles inhibits raising money through government bonds.

Notes to Chapter 3

1. As cited in William Watts and Lloyd A. Free, eds., *State of the Nation* (New York: Universe Books, 1973), pp. 33-35. This section draws heavily on that source, as well as Albert H. Cantril and Charles W. Roll, Jr., *Hopes and Fears of the American People* (New York: Universe Books, 1971), pp. 37-50.

2. *Asahi Evening News,* March 17, 1971.

3. Watts and Free, pp. 200-201.

4. *Yomiuri Shimbun* poll conducted by the American Institute of Public Opinion, September 17-21, 1971.

5. *1. U.S. Public Opinion toward Japan; 2. Image of Japan among U.S. University Students,* International Affairs Shiryo (Material) No. 109, Information and Cultural Affairs Bureau, Ministry of Foreign Affairs, March 15, 1973. Report based on polls conducted by the American Institute of Public Opinion.

6. Information drawn from a study in progress on the textile issue in U.S.-Japanese relations by I. M. Destler, Hideo Sato, and Haruhiro Fukui at the Brookings Institution, Washington, D.C.

7. Bernard C. Cohen, *The Press and Foreign Policy* (Princeton: Princeton University Press, 1965), p. 251.

8. Cohen, p. 75.

9. The number of front page articles on Japan has increased in this period by six to ten times.

10. Typical headlines during 1971-72 were: "Japan's Drive to Outstrip the United States," "Japan's Remarkable Industrial Machine," "Toward the Japanese Century," "Japan, Incorporated," and "Pearl Harbor in Reverse."

11. This fact is highlighted in Henry Rosovsky, ed., *Discord in the Pacific* (Washington, D.C.: Columbia Books, 1972). See the chapter by George R. Packard, "A Crisis in Understanding," pp. 142-143.

12. See, for example, John C. Donovan, *The Policy Makers* (New York: Pegasus, 1970), and Francis O. Wilcox, *Congress, the Executive and Foreign Policy* (New York: Harper and Row, 1971).

13. It should be noted that the differences between the House and Senate on agreement with executive budget requests for military spending lie in the committees rather than the bodies as a whole. The House Armed Services committee is more inclined to support Pentagon requests than is the House itself. Both Senate and House Appropriations Committees tend to scrutinize requests carefully and recommend cuts.

14. In recent years two major systems have been defeated in committee before reaching the floor: the Main Battle Tank and the Cheyenne helicopter.

15. Although he also consults regularly with the House Foreign Affairs Committee, there was no particular breach to be healed.

16. Decision making on Okinawa reversion is the subject of a study in progress by Priscilla Clapp and Haruhiro Fukui, The Brookings Institution, Washington, D.C.

17. There are some encouraging signs that the congressional base of knowledge on Japan is improving. As Alton Frye documents in "Con-

gress: The Virtues of its Vices," *Foreign Policy*, no. 3 (Summer 1971), p. 109, in recent years large numbers of foreign policy experts from the executive branch have sought employment on Capitol Hill, bringing new experience to bear on congressional attitudes toward foreign policy. A significant number of these "refugees" have had direct—and in some cases, extensive—experience with Japan. There have also been substantial efforts to provide congressmen themselves with direct exposure to Japan, although it would be impractical to try to document them here.

18. The State Department, the Joint Chiefs of Staff, the office of the Assistant Secretary of Defense for International Security Affairs, and the office of the Secretary of the Army.

19. For example, desire for the Republican nomination for President; a perceived need for securing permanent support from the Southern conservatives; the need to reward old friends for faithful political and financial support; maintaining a reputation for making good on promises.

20. President Nixon appears to have believed that Prime Minister Sato was powerful enough to single-handedly promise and deliver voluntary restrictions on Japanese exports and that Japan owed this to the United States in return for Okinawa.

Notes for Chapter 4

1. *Japan's Economy in 1980 in the Global Context* (Tokyo: Japan Economic Research Center, 1972).

Notes to Chapter 5

1. Henry Rosovsky, "Japan's Economic Future," *Challenge* (July–August 1973), p. 17.

2. For a more detailed analysis of what this trend develeration may look like after 1970, see ibid., pp. 15-17.

Notes to Chapter 7

1. This list points out the interesting, and perhaps coincidental, fact that all the summit meetings were held in Washington until 1970. The

two meetings in 1972 were convened by request of the United States and held at points closer to Japan—an indication of the end of the period of "pilgrimages." Incidentally, a Yoshida—Eisenhower meeting was held in 1954 prior to the Kishi—Eisenhower meeting. Another Tanaka—Nixon summit meeting in July—August 1973 was held after this chapter was written.

2. The full text can be found in Saito, Nagai, and Yamamoto, eds., *Sengoshiryo nichibeikankei* (U.S.-Japanese relations: Postwar references; Tokyo: Nihon Hyoronsha, 1970), pp. 71-72.

3. See, for example, "Yoshida no kaigai ryoko" (Yoshida's overseas tour), *Mainichi shimbun,* November 13, 1954, evening edition.

4. *Asahi shimbun,* November 12, 1954.

5. Ibid., June 23, 1957.

6. Ibid., June 21, 1957.

7. The full text of the communique can be found in the *Department of State Bulletin,* July 8, 1957, pp. 51-53.

8. *Asahi shimbun,* June 22, 1957.

9. *Ibid.,* June 22, 1957.

10. Edwin O. Reischauer, *Japan: Past and Present,* 3rd ed. rev., (Tokyo: Charles E. Tuttle, 1964), p. 283.

11. The Liberal Democratic Party won 296 seats, the Socialists 145, the Democratic Socialists 17, the Japan Communists 3, and the Independents 6.

12. The full text of the communique can be found in the *Department of State Bulletin,* July 10, 1961, pp. 57-58.

13. *Asahi shimbun,* June 25, 1961.

14. *Ibid.,* June 23, 1961.

15. The full text of the communique can be found in the *Department of State Bulletin,* February 1, 1965, pp. 134-136.

16. During the years following China's first nuclear test in October 1964, the Chinese nuclear "threat" had become a controversial subject in a series of U.S.-Japanese dialogues. Through my experience in these international academic conferences, I learned that U.S. scholars tended to stress the "threat," while their Japanese counterparts gave it less importance.

17. Testimony by George Ball before the Senate Foreign Relations Committee, April 7, 1965; statement issued by the U.S. Embassy in Tokyo, April 29, 1965; statement issued by the *Mainichi shimbun* editors, April 30, 1965; the protest by the president of the *Asahi shimbun* regarding the testimony of a high ranking U.S. official, May 1, 1965; statement issued by the U.S. Department of State regarding corrections on misunderstanding, May 1, 1965; as cited in *Sengoshiryo nichibeikankei,* pp. 382-384.

18. Minoru Omori's reports on North Vietnam had been carried in

the *Mainichi shimbun* since September 26, 1964; Ambassador Reischauer's remarks were made in his speech and a press conference afterwards in Osaka on October 5, 1964. He repeated his speech in Tokyo on October 25. Views expressed by the U.S. Department of State on Japan's press reports on Vietnam (October 7, 1964) and related references can be found in *Sengoshiryo nichibeikankei,* pp. 384-392.

19. Shigeharu Matsumoto, "Amerika no tomodachi eno tegami" (A letter to American friends), *Chuo Koron* (November 1965); Fuji Kamiya, "Nichibeikankei no genjo" (On the current state of U.S.-Japanese relations), *Chuo koron* (December 1965).

20. Premier Sato in his address of November 21, 1964, at a plenary session of the 47th Diet, said: "I would like to base our diplomacy on maintenance of peace, protection of freedom, advancement of *autonomous diplomacy* and contribution to improved global welfare." Two months later, in a policy address at the 48th Diet, he further elaborated: "I would like to promote *autonomous diplomacy* and pursue our safety and national interest to the fullest extent, while heading toward our supreme goal of the establishment and maintenance of world peace based on freedom and justice." (Italics are mine.) *Sato sori enzetsu shuroku* (Collection of Prime Minister Sato's addresses; Tokyo: Sorifu, 1970), pp. 24, 47.

21. *Sekaino nakano nihon keizai* (The Japanese economy in 1980 in the global context; Tokyo: Japan Economic Research Center, 1972), p. 30.

22. *Sato sori enzetsu shuroku,* p. 111.

23. Jun Eto, "Hawai kaigi no meian" (Light and shadow of the Hawaii conference) *Shokun,* (November 1972).

24. Gerald Curtis and Fuji Kamiya, eds., *Okinawa igono nichibeikankei* (U.S.-Japanese relations after Okinawa; Tokyo: Simul, 1970).

25. During this incident the authorities applied, for the first time, the regulations against mass meetings with arms.

26. The full text of the communique can be found in the *Department of State Bulletin,* December 4, 1967, pp. 744-747.

27. *Newsweek,* November 25, 1968.

28. A reporter called it the "Guam Doctrine," but in the following year it was renamed the "Nixon Doctrine" by President Nixon himself after he had been assured of its popularity among the U.S. public.

29. The full text of the communique can be found in the *Department of State Bulletin,* December 15, 1969, pp. 555-558.

30. United States Foreign Policy for the 1970's: The Emerging Structure of Peace, President Nixon's Report to Congress, February 9, 1972.

31. See, for example, the panel discussion by Jun Eto, Yonosuke

Nagai, and Fuji Kamiya in "Gaiko, geijitsu, senjitsu" (Diplomacy, art, and tactics), *Kikan geijyutsu* (Autumn 1971). Also, Yonosuke Nagai insists, from a slightly different angle, that U.S. actions were deliberate: "Nitchu kokko kaifuku no kyogi to shinjitsu" (Lies and truth in the restoration of Sino-Japanese relations) *Bungei shunji,* (February 1972). Similar views have been expressed by Graham T. Allison, "American Foreign Policy and Japan," in Henry Rosovsky, ed., *Discord in the Pacific* (Washington, D.C.: Columbia Books, 1972), as well as in a *New York Times* editorial of June 10, 1972.

32. Fuji Kamiya, "Haisenkoku nishi doitsu no gaiko nihon no gaiko" (Diplomacy of the vanquished: West German and Japanese diplomacy), *Shokun* (February 1973).

Notes to Chapter 8

1. The first major Sino-Japanese agreement after the joint communique was in fact a trade agreement signed in January 1974, although both sides had desired to give priority to the conclusion of a civil aviation agreement.

2. Other major problems on the priority list held no prospect for short-term solutions that could be undertaken before the approaching general election.

3. Article 8 of the Potsdam Proclamation states that "the Cairo Declaration shall be carried out." The Cairo Declaration in turn states that "All the territories Japan had stolen from the Chinese, such as Manchuria, Formosa, and the Pescadores, shall be restored to the Republic of China.

Notes to Chapter 9

1. China is acutely aware of the imperative of *Realpolitik,* and Chou En-lai has made clear to Prime Minister Tanaka that he did not object in principle to either the Japanese Fourth Defense Plan or to the Mutual Security Treaty with the United States—the latter presumably as insurance of a nonnuclear Japan.

2. The phrase is taken from *Gaiko seisho* (Diplomatic bluebook for 1971; Tokyo: Gaimusho, 1972), p. 103.

3. President Richard M. Nixon, *U.S. Foreign Policy for the 1970's: A Report to the Congress,* (Washington, D.C.: Government Printing Of-

fice, 1971), p. 13. The same statement also appeared in the President's first annual report in 1970.

4. Robert J. Pranger, *Defense Implications of International Indeterminacy*, (Washington, D.C.: American Enterprise Institute, 1972), *passim*.

5. For elaboration on immobilism in Japanese foreign policy making see Chapter 2 by Masataka Kosaka.

6. *Asahi shimbun*, January 18, 1973.

7. For an interesting discussion of the subjective links between Japan and the United States, see Hiroshi Kitamura, *Psychological Dimensions of U.S.-Japanese Relations*, (Cambridge, Mass.: Harvard University Center for International Affairs, 1971), *passim*.

8. Indeed, three Japanese newspapers (*Asahi shimbun, Nihon keizai shimbun*, and *Nishi nippon shimbun*) and the Kyodo News Agency had accepted in 1964 substantive controls (for example, no hostile reporting on the People's Republic of China) in order that their reporters could be stationed in Peking!

9. For elaboration on this point, see Chapter 11 in this collection by Morton Halperin .

10. See Chapter 10.

Notes to Chapter 10

1. "We must remember the only time in the history of the world that we have had any extended periods of peace is when there has been balance of power. It is when one nation becomes infinitely more powerful in relation to its potential competitor that the danger of war arises. So I believe in a world in which the United States is powerful. I think it will be a safer world and a better world if we have a strong, healthy United States, Europe, Soviet Union, China, Japan, each balancing the other, not playing one against the other, an even balance." *Time*, January 3, 1972.

2. See *East Asia and the World System: Part I: The Super-Powers and the Context*, Adelphi Paper No. 91, International Institute for Strategic Studies, November 1972, p. 40.

3. *U.S. Foreign Policy for the 1970's: Building for Peace. A Report to Congress* (Washington, D.C.: U.S. Government Printing Office, 1971).

4. See Zbigniew Brzezinski, *The Fragile Blossom: Crisis and Change in Japan* (New York: Harper and Row, 1972).

Notes to Chapter 11

1. George Kennan, "Japanese Security and American Policy," *Foreign Affairs* (October 1964), p. 24.

2. William J. Sebald, *With MacArthur in Japan,* (New York: W. W. Norton, 1965), pp. 80-82.

3. Hanson Baldwin, "Crisis in the Pacific," *The New York Times,* June 18, 1960.

4. William P. Bundy, "Asian Triangle," *Newsweek,* December 6, 1971.

Contributors

Priscilla Clapp is a research associate at the Brookings Institution, engaged in a study of decision making in U.S.-Japanese relations.

Morton Halperin, formerly a senior fellow at the Brookings Institution and deputy assistant secretary of defense (ISA), is currently engaged in a study of national security and constitutional procedures for the Twentieth Century Fund.

Donald Hellmann is professor of political science and Asian studies at the University of Washington. He is the author of *Japan and East Asia: the New International Order* (1972) and other works.

Tadao Ishikawa is a professor at Keio University, specializing in Chinese studies.

Masataka Kosaka is a professor on the Faculty of Law, Kyoto University, and research chief of the Japan Institute of International Affairs.

Fuji Kamiya is a professor of international affairs at Keio University, and research chief of the Japan Institute of International Affairs.

Hisao Kanamori, formerly with Japan's Economic Planning Agency, is now president of the Japan Economic Research Center in Tokyo.

Dwight Perkins is professor of modern China studies and of economics at Harvard University and associate director of the East Asian Research Center at Harvard University.

Edwin O. Reischauer, formerly U.S. ambassador to Japan, is now University Professor at Harvard. He is the author of numerous books on Japan and U.S.-Japanese relations.

Henry Rosovsky is professor of economics at Harvard University and dean of the Faculty of Arts and Sciences of Harvard College.

Kiichi Saeki, formerly the director of the National Defense College, is now the president and executive director of the Nomura Research Institute of Technology and Economics in Japan.